Waters of Tyne

by

T. H. Rowland

To Gwen

**Sandhill
Press**

First Published by T.H. Rowland in 1991.
This reprint published in 1994.
© T.H. Rowland.

Sandhill Press Ltd.,
17 Castle Street,
Warkworth, Morpeth,
Northumberland, NE65 0UW

ISBN 0 946098 36 0

Cover photograph : Detail of *'Newcastle from St. Ann's'* 1835 by J.W. Carmichael
with the kind permission of Tyne & Wear Museums Service.

Acknowledgements:

Thanks to my wife for the typing.
To Northumberland County Library and Northumberland County Record Office
for help and information.
Newcastle Central Library for the photograph of Alston.
The Laing Gallery for the Pre-Raphaelite Exhibition.
To Councils and Information Offices on the way.

Printed by The Abbey Press, Hexham.

CONTENTS

3

FEATHERSTONE, Bellister and Blenkinsop Castles.
Haltwhistle — church, towers and market.
Willimoteswick and the Ridleys.
Beltingham and Anthony Hedley.
Ridley Hall and grounds.
Tyne Floods of 1771 — devastation and rebuilding of bridges.
Exploring Allen Waters Cupola and leadmining.
Whitfield Hall and Churches. Langley — Allenheads — Allendale.
South Tyne continued. Haydon Bridge — Newbrough — Fourstones.
Waters meet at Warden.

Chapter 4. THE RIVER TYNE
HEXHAM — Monastery and Market Town. Middle March Centre.
St. John Lee. Acomb. Beaufront Castle.
DILSTON and Devil's Water. Tragic Earl of Derwentwater.
Diversion to Blanchland — Model Village.
CORBRIDGE and Corstopitum — Roman town, Anglo Saxon Church
and Vicar's Pele.
BYWELL ON TYNE — Hall, ruined castle, two Anglo Saxon churches.
A town that disappeared and important fishery.
Stocksfield and Riding Mill.
Thomas Bewick and Cherryburn. Prudhoe Castle and Fishery.
Ovingham and Wylam. Railways and Railway engineers.
Heddon and Newburn. Industries. Swalwell and Winlaton.
Ryton Village.

Chapter 5. THE RIVER DERWENT
The Derwentwater Reservoir. Edmundbyers. Muggleswick.
Consett Ironworks. Shotley Bridge and Ebchester.
Derwent Valley — walks on the old railway and through parks.
Chopwell. Hamsterley. Lintzford and Gibside. Whickham.
Axwell Park. Derwent haugh. Dunston and Industry. Team Valley.

Chapter 6. NORTH OF THE TYNE
Benwell, Denton and the Roman Wall.
Elswick and Armstrong's Works.
NEWCASTLE UPON TYNE. River and Bridges. Fortress and Port.
History of the Quayside and the Town.
The Great Fire from across the Tyne. 1854.
Ships and Ballast: improvement of Navigation. Collingwood.
The Scott brothers. Bessie Surtees House: English Heritage.
Important Buildings. Bridges. Hospitals and Museums.
Castle — All Saints Church — St. Nicholas (Cathedral) and
other Churches. Town Walls.
Grainger, Dobson and Clayton — building developments.
1929 Exhibition. Modern developments — Civic Centre, Art Gallery.

List of Illustrations

Introduction

Water of Tyne

O you who drink my cooling waters clear
Forget not the far hills from whence they flow,
Where over fell and moor, and year by year.
Spring, summer, autumn, winter come and go,
With showering sun and rain and storm and snow.
Where over the green bents forever blow
The four free winds of heaven: where time falls
In solitary places calm and slow,
Where pipes the curlew and the plover calls
Beneath an open sky my waters spring,
Beneath the clear sky welling fair and sweet
A draught of coolness for your throat to bring,
A sound of coolness in the busy street.

> *Inscribed on the fountain in Hexham Market and*
> *written by Wilfrid W. Gibson, the poet born in*
> *Hexham in 1878.*

Rivers, in a sense, are movements in time. For ages they have been making the landscape, removing and depositing material. They have been harnessed to provide power for corn mills. In leadmines and ironworks streams of water have been used for power and transport of materials.

The river Tyne has several sources. The South Tyne begins in Cumbria: the North Tyne and Rede emerge on the Scottish Border. The waters of South Tyne disappear underground and emerge in gullies, caverns and lead mine workings. Water was collected in reservoirs and released, forming "hushes" to expose lead bearing veins of rock. North Tyne waters have been held by weirs to provide drinking water for thirsty Tyneside.

Here is a continuing cycle of change. Mist, rain and snow make their deposits on the hills. Waters may flow north to the Liddel and Jed streams, south to Rede or North Tyne. From Cross Fell they may make the South Tyne, the Eden or the Tees.

From time immemorial there have been migrations of salmon, sea trout and eels. They provided food for man, especially in medieval times when fish were so important to monasteries. Fishing was not a sport, but essential to survival. There were numerous fisheries and places for wildfowl, another source of food. For centuries these were turbulent territories with armies and raiders passing one way or another. The men of Tynedale and Redesdale had a bad reputation, and Newcastle masters were forbidden to take them, or Scots, as apprentices *because the parties there brought up are known by education or nature not to be of honest conversation: they commit frequent thefts and other felonies, proceeding from such lewde and wicked progenitors.*

7

This book follows the course of the Tyne waters down to the sea. It is intended neither as a guide book nor a history, but a river journey recording what emerges from the past or from the present, and mainly from the activities of man through time. There is so much involved that it must be selective and impressionistic, but always recording the observations of previous visitors and inhabitants. Most important are communcations and crossings of the water. The rivers determined the line of roads and railways and even the location of Hadrian's Wall.

Mark Akenside, Newcastle born poet and surgeon, wrote —

> *O ye dales*
> *Of Tyne and ye most ancient woodlands; where*
> *Oft as the giant flood obliquely strides*
> *And his banks open and his lawns extend*
> *Stops short the pleased traveller to view*
> *Presiding o'er the scene some rustic tower*
> *Founded by Norman or by Saxon hands.*
>
> *From 'Pleasures of the Imagination.' (1757)*

Sir Walter Scott, in 1792 wrote

There are several lakes among the mountains above Hexham, well worth going miles to see. They are surrounded by old towers and castles in situations most savagely romantic. What would I have given to have been able to take off pieces of some them!

This was how he built his house at Abbotsford. He saw Northumberland as a land of castles and romance.

Overlooking the Tyne are many Anglo Saxon church towers and Norman castles as well as numerous strongholds of a later date.

The river echoes —

> *For men may come and men may go,*
> *But I go on for ever.*
>
> *Alfred Lord Tennyson, 'The Brook'.*

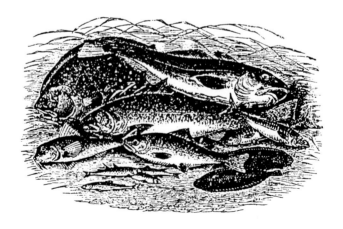

Chapter One
REDEWATER

The most northerly source of water of Tyne is that which supplies the River Rede. This emerges from a group of small streams beneath Carter Bar, where at 1370 feet above sea level the main road crosses the Scottish Border. It is now a scenic stop for travellers, who are photographed beneath a huge monolith inscribed England on the north side and Scotland on the south. There are extensive views in both directions, and the road was formerly used by raiders. In 1575 it was the scene of the Redeswire Fray. Sir John Forster, English Warden of the Middle Marches, and Sir John Carmichael, deputy keeper of Liddlesdale, met to settle differences according to custom. But fighting broke out between the men of Jedburgh and Tynedale. Several men were killed and some prisoners taken by the Scots as well as some 600 cattle.

Sheep and cattle-stealing ceased in time, but it is surprising to discover that in 1886 on a moonlight night in November, there was trouble with a gang of salmon poachers. Twenty six of them came with spears and farmyard forks to take salmon but they were met by six stout water bailiffs armed with cudgels and truncheons. There was severe fighting and heavy blows exchanged, but the poachers were driven back towards Jedburgh.

Water flows from Redeswire, north into Scotland and south into England. From a height, the Rede appears as a thread beneath the frowning hills on both sides. The slopes are steep and the herbage scant. Records can be read of *All those summerings called Catcleugh* — that is they were summer pastures only. On a hill called Coomsdon, poor coal was found and used for fuelling lime kilns. The lime was sent over the Border into Scotland. The great change in the present century is that the water of Rede has been dammed to form the Catcleugh Reservoir, a great alteration to the landscape.

A century ago Edmund Bogg in his *Wanderings in Border Country* wrote; *Still upwards, past Ramshope, the hills rising ridge above ridge, until the world is hushed into repose in this lonely region and light fleecy clouds skim the mountains, giving grand and varied effect of light and shadow. At Whitlee Farm the Rede has narrowed to a mere streamlet trickling down the slopes of Carter Fell, over which the road winds, and suddenly there spreads before the traveller a rich swelling landscape, whose varied loveliness language can scarcely describe.* On a return journey later he wrote, *On the southern side of the valley gangs of navvies were busily employed in laying a line of huge pipes from upper Redesdale to carry water to Newcastle. A warm rush along the Roman Road and we found Woodburn disturbed by a number of navvies in the midst of drunken saturnalia.*

Woodburn was the centre for the construction of the waterworks since it was on the railway to Redesmouth, and had connections with Hexham to the south and Deadwater to the north. It also had a link with Morpeth and was used to supply troops training on the Otterburn Range. Additionally a three feet guage railway was constructed along the line of the pipe to bring supplies of stone and other materials. This line ran from the dam site at Catcleugh to a lower reservoir at Hallington. The railway had seven locomotives and two fixed engines. By 1895 the pipeline was completed and water flowed to Hallington, and thence to Whittle and the populated areas of Tynedale.

1. Catcleugh Reservoir on the Rede.

Catcleugh Reservoir

To complete the dam and reservoir at Catcleugh was much more prolonged and difficult. The main problem was the height of the dam, and whether or not a fish pass could be constructed. There were powerful sporting interests among the landowners, who had to be compensated for losses as well as paid a high price for the land to be used. Ramshope and Whitlee farms were purchased and compensation paid for fishing rights, so the work could begin.

Large gangs of labourers were needed and in 1899 below the site there were 47 huts, housing 331 men, 70 woman and 94 children. Numbers were increased for workers from 400 to 600 or more. 20 horses were employed and six railway engines. There were 26 steam powered excavators. The embankment of the dam was 510 feet wide and 85 feet high and there was a tunnel for the river to flow through until the dam was finished.

The work was at last completed in 1905 and the equipment sold. These activities had increased the population of the area and made it, for a time, an industrial site.

The Rede pipeline took water directly to reservoirs at Colt Crag and Swinburn: they were linked to two more reservoirs at Hallington, which were connected with Whittle Dean, the original reservoir near Welton, completed in 1848, mainly on land from the Duke. A castellated house designed by Dobson overlooks the reservoirs, now the haunts of fisherman and wildfowl. The

Whittington tunnel and Pont aqueduct had been completed so that the water could flow down. On the north side of the Military Road a mushroom-shaped fountain shows where the water is emerging with great force. From here it settles into reservoirs and filter beds.

Meanwhile we have to return to the Rede. The Catcleugh Reservoir and its works have now mellowed into the landscape and the valley attractive with a variety of trees. In autumn time the coloured leaves are specially picturesque. Associated with the reservoir is the village of Byrness, which has become a forestry village with the development of the Redesdale Forest. The old village is made up of a few stone houses and a charming little church, which dates back to the end of the eighteenth century, built through the efforts of the Revd. L. Dutens of Elsdon. It was built in local stone on an elevated prehistoric site overlooking the Rede, It contains a window 'In memory of those men, women and children who have died during the construction of the reservoir of Catcleugh'. The window was erected by fellow workmen and friends: 64 names are inscribed on a brass plate. The glass window depicts workmen with barrows, picks and shovels. A steam engine with its wagons is shown and a little girl sits waiting and watching with her father's 'bait' wrapped in a handkerchief.

The reservoir drained some 10,000 acres and held 2,305 million gallons of water. It could easily supply 10 million gallons of water a day. Batinghope Burn which flows into the reservoir was the place of the sad story of Percy Reed of Troughend, murdered by the Croziers and betrayed by the Halls of Girsonfield while hunting. A ballad of the incident is called the Death of Percy Reed.

The A68 keeps close to the course of the River Rede, and to the north is a military area. It was also a military area in Roman times, and south of Rochester, the Roman Road called Dere Street, leaves the line of the present road. There was a whole series of forts and temporary camps from Bremenium (Rochester) to Chew Green on the Scottish Border. The Roman fort at Rochester can be reached by turning off the main road at the old school, where the porch is built of Roman stone and decorated with two ballista balls.

At Horsley, further south is a Neo Norman Church, designed by J. and B. Green 1844. It contains a Roman altar from one of the forts, which was dedicated to Victory and Peace.

On the other side of the road with the area of the Redesdale Experimental Farm is the deserted medieval village of Evistones. It contained a number of strong houses or bastles, now in ruins, but the vaulted basement of one still stands. All these things are reminders of the dangerous past of this area.

At Elishaw the A68 crosses the Rede on an iron bridge, while the other road continues along the Rede towards Otterburn, Hereabouts, in August 1388, was fought the historic battle by moonlight between the men of Percy and Douglas, far famed in ballad and story. The battle was re-enacted in 1988 by modern exponents of war-gaming. A standing stone in a conifer plantation marks the place where Douglas is supposed to have fallen.

Otterburn

In Otterburn is a modern military camp. The most attractive places in the

11

village are the Otterburn Arms Hotel and Otterburn Towers, now an hotel. It contains within its structure some masonry of the medieval tower house, but it is mostly reconstructed. At one time it was the residence of Howard Pease, author of Northumberland's Decameron and other writings. The water of the Rede at Otterburn was used to drive the machinery of Otterburn Woollen Mill, which dates from 1821 and is still run by the same family of Waddell. Tweed is no longer manufactured here, but the showrooms provide a wide range of quality materials for visitors to purchase.

2. Monument on the site of the Battle of Otterburn.

Below Otterburn the River Rede is joined by the Elsdon Burn, which descends from the military area of Otterburn by Elsdon Mill and Castle. The castle is a motte and bailey type which was never built up in stone. The vicar's pele, a medieval fortified tower, stands high on the other side of the stream and road. There is an interesting medieval church, where dead from the Battle of Otterburn were buried. The village is built round a large green, on which is the old circular stone built pound, once used for keeping stray animals. The Elsdon area has seen as considerable amount of ooal mining, but the last pit has been closed.

The waters of the Rede have made a winding valley to East and West Woodburn. Farming consists of rearing cattle and sheep with very little arable farming. In past times there was more local corn grown and there were as many as 12 mills in the area. When better roads were built coal was carried over the Scottish Border in exchange for corn. There is now opencast mining on Raylees Common to the east of the Rede, where the land is pock-marked with old bell pits.

The main road to the west of the river is Dere Steet, the old Roman Road with camps at Blakehope and Dargues. The earthworks can still be traced in the fields. But Percy Reed's bastle at Troughend has been demolished. Edmund Bogg passed this way - *forward along the Roman road where the quietude of the night is broken by the boisterous laughter and shouts of the navvies, whilst from the huts the highway is flooded with a ruddy light.* Nowadays the noise is heavy motor traffic, usually travelling at high speed, and it is pleasant to divert to Corsenside, where stands a lonely church in what was once a large parish. It stands on an elevated site overlooking the Rede and has a large collection of tombstones in the churchyard, many of Halls and Reeds, the leading families. One monument, like one at Elsdon, takes the form of a fine Georgian portal. The original church was strongly built in Norman style, but windows were altered in the eighteenth century. There are a number of old grave slabs kept within the church, which is maintained as a redundant building and only used occasionally for meetings. There was a candlelight service and music for the Otterburn 500 celebrations in 1988. A large farmhouse, near the church, has a date of 1660.

Very fine views are seen from Corsenside and still more from the scenic lay-by on high ground before descent into West Woodburn. To the west of the road there stands a Roman milestone that was re-erected by the Redesdale Society. These stones marked the Roman miles on the main road to Scotland. There is another Roman milestone at Waterfalls, a farm on the distant horizon to the south beyond Fourlaws, where was a Roman camp. East of the road a track leads down to the River Rede with its old bridge and attractive fringes of trees. Looking southwards it can be seen that the line of Dere street leaves the present road and leads directly to the Roman fort of Risingham (Habitancum) on the other side of the Rede. It stands up as a rectangular enclosure which is surrounded by a series of banks and ditches. It was built of stone and strongly fortified, but spoiled by local stone robbers. It has not been fully excavated - only a few exploratory trenches establish dimensions, gateways and internal buildings.

3. Ruins of Ridsdale Ironworks.

13

The houses at West Woodburn line both sides of the street, and a road eastwards leads along the Rede to East Woodburn. Here once was the hall of the Lisle family, but it has gone to ruin.

Further along the main road southwards can be seen the area of the railway station and the quarry. Also there can be seen in the distance the spoil heaps of the Ridsdale iron mines. Here there were important ironworks, used by William Armstrong. These works started in 1864 and were discontinued in 1879. The engine house of the works still stands in stone and is often mistaken by travellers for a castle. The Woodburns are interesting to explore, and towards East Woodburn one farm building contains a Roman altar. The church of All Saints was built in in 1906-7, pleasantly situated within sound of the waters of the River Rede, which flows under the bridge westwards in its way to meet the North Tyne.

Risingham Roman fort can be reached by a field road west of the main road and in this area is the rock of Park Head, which was carved into a figure called "Robin of Risingham". The rock stood about eight feet high and the figure four feet high, with a panel above it as if intended for an inscription. The figure was depicted (according to Horsley's description) as a huntsman in a belted tunic. His raised right hand carries a bow and in his left dangles a hare. He has a drape about his shoulders and a quiver on his back. He would seem to be a Roman god of hunting, with the name of Silvanus or others depending on the location. For this reason he has been likened to Robin Hood or an Umfraville called Robin of Redesdale. In local legend he became a giant and is mentioned by Sir Walter Scott in *Ivanhoe* and *Rokeby*. In fact the carving became so famous that the local farmer got fed up with visitors and removed the upper parts of the rock to make gateposts. Only Robin's legs remained, and these can still be seen. Mackenzie wrote — *a churlish Goth has entirely destroyed this curious remain of antiquity*, and Scott writes that a sulky churlish boor has destroyed the ancient statue.

Curiously enough the destroyer was named John Shanks, the remaining legs preserving his name!

There has been some speculation about Roman navigation of Northumberland rivers and whether Risingham could be supplied by water. Evidence is that the river has shifted considerably — Camden said it was washing away the north walls and Mackenzie wrote that a Mr Reed of the Crag, an adjoining proprietor had removed a lot of stone whether from the walls or bridge, using them to embank the river. So erections in Roman stone do not mean that the work took place in Roman times. Roman stone was used in other buildings.

Mackenzie wrote: *There are no splendid mansions in this parish. The houses of the lairds generally consist of two kitchens, a parlour and two rooms above. Three or four of them still inhabit the Peels, or strong houses of their ancestors.*

Examples of this kind can be seen at Low Leam and at Hole, where the house stands to full height and is still used for farm purposes, with animals living in the tunnel vaulted basement. The upper quarters, once inhabited by the farming family, are used as a store, and there is a loft storey above. The building is strongly built and stands four square. The basement is barrel vaulted and here was the original entry. The outside steps to the first floor were added at a later

4. Hole Bastle on the River Rede.

date. It is an eloquent reminder of life in Redesdale in medieval times. Some of the stone may well have been taken from Roman Risingham as well as material for field walls. The area is now very sparsely populated, and the land is mostly used for rearing sheep. There has been mining for coal and quarrying of stone, especially ironstone. The Redesmouth railway passed south of the river from West Woodburn and was linked with local industries. There are a number of native sites in this area, including Buteland and Rede Bridge. I came to excavate here before the railway closed, getting off the Hexham train at Redesmouth. Here was a double length of track and the north bound train had to wait for the one coming south at an easy pace. It was a long haul northwards and powerful locomotives had to be used for the pull to Riccarton and Hawick beyond the Border. Noise echoed through the valley, but now industry has gone — ironworks from Bellingham as well as Ridsdale and coal pits have closed; there is peace broken by calls of sheep and curlew.

Redesmouth

There is an interesting walk along the narrow lanes here and over the old Rede Bridge - hump backed with two arches. The railway viaduct across the Rede has been demolished, but the road bridge beside it has been widened. There are beautiful views of the river and sounds of the water. Above on either hand the railway embankments come to an abrupt end, where the viaduct disappeared. There were station buildings and engine sheds above. Old photographs here of steam trains have great appeal to railway enthusiasts, and one regrets that this line could not be kept open. At one time trains ran on Sunday Garden Excursions on a route from Newcastle - Hexham - Redesmouth - Woodburn - Knowsgate - Scots Gap - Middleton - Meldon and Morpeth, then back to Newcastle. Below Redesmouth, the Rede joins the North Tyne; a river junction near

15

a former railway junction. We can return by imaginary train to Deadwater and the origins of the North Tyne in the hills of the Border. Deadwater Station, now disused, is on the English side of the Border in an area covered with trees and part of the Kielder Forest, the largest man made forest in Britain.

5. River Rede near Redesmouth.

6. Redesmouth old Railway Bridge.

Chapter Two
THE NORTH TYNE

7. The North Tyne below Deadwater.

The North Tyne has its origin between Kielder and Saughtree stations, in what was wide moorland and waste, land long disputed between the English and the Scots. Peel Fell, reaching a height of 1975 feet overlooks the area, with views in all directions and waters seemingly undecided where to go, hence the name of Deadwater.

Mackenzie wrote — 'a moss or morass extended across the Border into Scotland, containing a sulphurous spring' and the comment was added from an earlier visitor — "it only wantes proper accommodation to make Deadwater a place of more resort', in other words a spa. Armstrong's Map (1769 has 'Bath and Spa Well'.

It can be a forbidding place with stern and dark hued hills, but on other days it can be attractive with feelings of fresh air and freedom. *Amidst the dark billowy moors to the confines of Deadwater and Black Fell where in the sunless sykes and ravines the North Tyne has its source, the snow still remained deep in the ridges, thought it was the month of May* (Bogg).

From Peel Fell the sea can be seen both east and west. High on Peel Fell is the Kielder Stone, a well known landmark standing 26 feet high and measuring 46 feet across. It is supposed to be a monument to the Cout or Colt of Kielder, a great fighter and hero of many battles. He was only killed when the men of Lord Soulis of Hermitage held him under water with their lances. There was in fact a Sir William Knout who died between 1289 and 1291 in the time of Edward I, who called here in 1296. The Wheel Way was an important mediaeval road, which was later used by cattle drovers. It was once thought to be Roman, but this is no longer acceptable. There was a hospital and chapel of Quele or Whele. King Edward III stayed there in 1347, when areas of Scotland were ruled by the English King. The Kielder Stone is said to have been used as an unofficial post office, and missives and other things were hidden here. it was unlucky to ride round it three times 'withershins' i.e. the opposite way to the sun.

Bogg, again on his way, saw *Peel Fell and Carter Fell, wreathed in a curtain of vapour, now rising, now dispersing, creeping and curling so mysteriously around the brown of the stern, sullen mountains, where the tempest shrieks and howls and torrents leap through the ravines in uncontrollable fury.*

In the times of Border warfare, the lords on either side depended upon men to serve them, and there were more of them than the land could support by farming. People tended to move away and these lands became depopulated and villages deserted. In the latter part of the seventeenth century the Earl of Northumberland wanted North Tyne and Kielder to be repopulated. But developments tended towards the establishment of large sheep farms. The landlords had a great interest too in hunting, shooting and fishing. Hunting Lodges were set up by Sir John Swinburne at Mounces, and the Duke of Northumberland at Kielder — the Castle.

From 1762 to 1779 the Duke was in dispute with Douglas as in past centuries over the boundaries of their estates, which was the Border. Armstrong's Map drawn for the Duke, has areas marked 'disputed'. This was settled in 1779 and boundary stones were set up with N for Northumberland on the south side and D for Douglas, somehow reversed, on the north side. Three hundred years after the Battle of Otterburn the old ballads were being resurrected, but the protagonists of Percy and Douglas were now at peace.

Kershope Castle, on or near the Border, has disappeared and 'ruins' were recorded on the old maps, as were those of Bell's Chapel. Bell's Burn to the west of Deadwater was the Border for part of its course, and Bell's Kirk was a meeting place. In 1715 there was but 'a mean village...where are the ruins of an old chapel'. Kielder, the rushing water, meets the North Tyne at Kielder Castle and greatly increases the flow.

Kielder Castle

The first Duke of Northumberland came to live at Alnwick Castle, and a survey was made of all his estates. Anthony Armstrong was commissioned to make a great map of Northumberland, which is still a most valuable record of the County in 1769. The Duke was much concerned with the improvement of his estates, planting trees and adding 'eyecatchers' or follies to the landscape. Kielder Castle can be regarded as one of these, but is has a purpose — a base for sporting activities. The historian John Hodgson has recorded the event. *Earl Percy and his companions went to Kielder and fixed upon the ground to erect a house for moor game hunting, and in 1772 the foundation was laid and the building begun according to the design of his Grace the Duke of Northumberland. It was finished in 1755 and named Kielder Castle. In August 1777 the Earl with Mr Williams and Mr Bertram Mitford passed ten days at the Castle where his lordship entertained the herds and girls with a collation and dances, distributing ribbons among the lasses. In August 1799 Lord and Lady Percy with the Earl of Aylsford, Governor Gare, Mr Charlton and Mr Williams passed three weeks at Kielder where a collation and dance were repeated.*

This seems very different from what Sir Walter Scott told Macaulay — *The women had no other dress than a bed gown and petticoat. The men were savage and could hardly be brought to rise from the heath...They (the women) sung a wild tune, the burthen of which was 'Ourina, Ourina, Ourina'. The females sang, the men danced round and at a certain part of a tune they drew their dirks, which they always wore.*

Mackenzie reported *A memorable match at the football took place near Kielder Castle, about the year 1790. A vast concourse of people assembled from Liddisdale, on the Scotch side of the Border, and from the pastoral vale of North Tyne. Twenty were chosen by the people of each of the districts of play three games. The contest was carried on with inconceivable eagerness until the end of the fourth game, each party having won twice: but the North Tyne got the fifth and were declared victors. Some of the players were so completely exhausted as to be unable to walk home: and a few, who died soon afterwards, dated the commencement of their illness from that day.*

8. The Kielder Railway Viaduct.

Kielder Castle was built around a courtyard with an arched entrance and main buildings with battlements and Gothic windows — the taste of the Duke. The grounds were planted with mixed timbers as at Alnwick. The Castle was taken over in the 1930's with many acres of land by the Forestry Commission, and this was the beginning of the present Kielder Forest which has spread over a huge area of 180 square miles.

19

When the North British Railway extended its line to Riccarton in 1862, to gain the approval of the Duke of Northumberland, the Kielder Viaduct had to be built in appropriate castellar style with turrets and battlements. A century later with the development of Kielder Water as a reservoir, the bridge was preserved as a fine example of our industrial heritage. The railway was an essential part of industrial development, but before this landowners had been building roads for the benefits of their estates.

Sir John Swinburne had his shooting lodge at Mounces, and did a great deal to improve communcations. Hodgson was told that he had built a dozen bridges over the tributaries of the North Tyne, and many miles of road were laid by him.

No previous communication existed between the North Tyne and Scotland, now carriages of every description travel this way with perfect ease. No coals are to be had in the adjoining part of Liddesdale and it was supplied very scantily from a colliery on the North Tyne not far from Kielder, that were conveyed thither only in summer, on horseback. A colliery is now opened on the Lewisburn, that supplies a large district in Scotland, even as far as Hawick and even to Jedburgh. This road now provides a walk along the Lewisburn to the Scottish Border at Bloody Bush. A 20 feet stone pillar marks the Border and carries information on the toll charges levied when it was a toll road. The coming of the railway greatly facilitated the transport of people, animals and all kinds of freight — coal, stone and timber.

From 1862 there was a Plashetts Coal Company working with varying success, and by 1889 there was a village with 64 houses. Travel and transport was by train. There was a chapel and a school. The colliery had steam engine, blacksmiths and joiner's shops and a brickworks. The strike of 1926 finished it as a going concern; Kielder woods and Kielder Water have eventually buried it, and only the memory remains. Kielder Water can provide electricity to take the place of steam.

The Kielder Reservior

The developments, which concerned Redesdale Water, were carried out by the Newcastle and Gateshead Water Company. They had thought of using the North Tyne, but nothing had been done about it. The present project was undertaken by Northumbrian Water with the support of other authorities. It would provide for Wearside and Teesside as well as Tyneside at a time when serious water shortages were threatened. The North Tyne was suitable because of the nature of the land and the lack of population. Also it could supply the regions estimated requirements. The development of Kielder Forest had lessened the natural attractions of the area. The reservoir would mean the removal of many trees as well as changing roads, so it would at least add to the variety of the landscape. After two enquiries, it was granted Parliamentary permission in 1974.

About 1½ million trees had to be felled and the stumps buried. Twenty-six houses had to be built to house those whose properties were affected. Finance was provided for the investigation of 21 archaeological sites that might be affected and the Kielder Viaduct was preserved. A new North Tyne road had to be built above the valley floor, and altogether it was a gigantic operation. 8½ miles in length it was designed to create a scenic route. Many water courses had to be crossed, and three large bridges built — the largest over the Lewisburn and the most dramatic at Mounces. The forest trees were cut and pruned to provide an attractive background. Curves were made to suit the contours of the land and the arc of the large dam. This consists of an embankment rising to a height of 170 feet and extending about ¾ mile in length. There is a road across it to the car park, protected by a parapet wall. A special wave wall was built at the top of the dam for extra protection, since in a strong wind the waves are very pulsating. The area near the dam is forbidden to any kind of boating. Millions of tons of clay were needed to seal the dam and the bed of the reservoir. It is 7 miles long and measures 27½ miles round the perimeter with a capacity of 44 billion gallons of water. It is the largest man-made lake in Britian carved out of the largest man-made forest and considerably bigger than Ullswater.

9. The Kielder Reservoir.

A dominating feature of the dam, until water was admitted, was the valve tower, standing 212 feet high. Water can be drawn off at four different levels, emerging into a concrete culvert at the base of the tower. Beyond the northern end of the dam is an overflow weir, which allows surplus water to flow into the North Tyne and can provide against sudden floods. Water power is used to generate electricity, and two turbo generators have been installed.

Five miles northwards is the second dam, at Bakethin, the upper end of the lake. Its main purpose was to cover mudflats that might be exposed when water was withdrawn. The Bakethin dam stands 56 feet high and is 541 feet long, and ensures that there will always be water here. It is a conservation area, and there is a stretch of water ideal for fishing. A Kielder salmon hatchery has been established to compensate for lost spawning grounds above the weirs.

In three years, more than a million salmon have been released into the North Tyne to immigrate to the sea to feed, returning to the river as adult salmon to spawn. This has only been made possible by the cleaning of the river, an achievement of Northumbria Water.

21

Work on the Kielder dam took 4½ years, and the flooding of the valley took a further 2 years. On May 26th, 1982 Kielder Water, which had cost £167 millions, was opened by the Queen. Water from Kielder flows down the North Tyne 36 miles to Riding Mill, where is situated Britain's largest pumping station. It can move some 240 million gallons of water a day, to either Tyneside or the Tees and the Wear. Curiously enough Kielder village consumes none of this water, it relies on spring water piped from Deadwater Fell.

Since the demand for water has not been so great as expected, Kielder Water has become much more important as recreational site. All kinds of water activities are provided — sailing, boating, canoeing, water ski-ing and cruises. There are many parking and picnic sites in various places. Forest walks and drives are possible. There is a toll route through to Byrness on the Carter Bar route. At Tower Knowe is the main information centre for Kielder Water and at Kielder Castle is the museum and information centre for Kielder Forestry. There are special areas for camping and exploration — the Scouts have a camp at Hawkirst. It is also possible to view the disused railway and the Kielder Viaduct. There are facilities for bird-watching as well as fishing, and forest animals may be seen. Painters and photographers can admire the hills, the trees and reflections in the water. By using the Ferry cruises visitors can make a complete circuit of the waters or drop off at different places for walking or browsing. Cycles can be hired for riding the tracks.

For contrast to the present we can turn to Mackenzie (1825).

The banks of the Kielder in ancient times have been clothed with wood: and the adjoining country, although bleak and barren, has been enriched and beautified with thick groves. Some vestiges yet remain of the decayed woods...About 20 years ago, the shepherds set fire to the heath on a hill near a place called Yarrow, which the weather being dry, communicated to an extensive peat moss and exposed the remains of an ancient forest of pine. The people of the neighbourhood go to this place, called Firtree Moss for wood for ladders etc. and make torches of it, which they use in taking salmon with fish spears in the night. Yarrow is at the south end of Kielder Water, and the road leads down the valley towards Falstone.

Stephen Oliver, in his *Rambles* published in 1835, gives another account of how salmon were caught. The locals used a kind of double boat called 'trows', for use in the river where the fish could not be taken by net. Two narrow boats were joined at the prow, but separated at the stern by a flat board. The boats were long, light and narrow almost like canoes, but strengthened inside by thwarts. Two men took part in the fishing — one the steersman operated by a pole from the stern, the other stood amidships with one foot in each boat. He had a pronged spear, called a 'leister', and waited for the sight of a salmon — striking in the middle or on either side of the trows. Trows were pushed out into pools to accustom salmon to them. They were only used by daylight in the fishing season, but no doubt some poachers operated by night, using lights.

The North Tyne above Bellingham was famous for poachers, who did not confine their attentions to fish. They helped themselves to grouse and other wildfowl as well as animals such as hares and rabbits. The salmon poachers were not confined to their own waters, but helped themselves from the Coquet. They beat off the Rothbury watchers on one occasion and came back with four horse-loads of fish.

There was also good fishing for pike in both Rede and North Tyne. Kielder water was considered to be one of the best streams in the county. It was interesting to see that at this time, the men of Tyne and Rede confined their activities to poaching and not to sheep stealing or cattle lifting. They might be involved in brawls at local fairs or cockfights, but not in fighting as in Border warfare. The landscape and the waters were also changing. The landowners were much concerned about their hunting shooting and fishing. Oliver recorded that after the Bywell weir was lowered about 1832, many more salmon and other fish were seen in the North Tyne. Pike and otters competed with the anglers for catches.

It might here be noticed that today, though salmon can no longer come up to Kielder, because of the dam, a hatchery here compensates for the loss of spawning grounds. This will continue after the privatisation of the Water Industry. The National Rivers Authority will take over the hatchery and be responsible for stocking Tyne waters with young salmon.

The hatchery opened in 1972, and in ten years it has reared more than 3 million fish. Before the dam was built, it was estimated that there were some 40,000 salmon above Kielder, and it was intended to stock the Tyne with 160,000 salmon annually. Other rivers are supplied with salmon. Sea trout are also reared, and the Reservoir is stocked with brown trout. Salmon tagged at Kielder have been caught as far away as the Faroes and Greenland. So the saga of the salmon continues.

More recently a French firm called Lyonnaise des eaux has taken over the Newcastle and Gateshead and the Sunderland and South Shields Water Companies under the privatisation scheme.

Falstone

Below the Kielder Reservoir the valley widens and there is a different look among the trees; the native oaks, ashes and alders pre-dominate. The village of Falstone comes into view. It is reached by crossing a three-arched bridge, built over the North Tyne in 1844 to replace a ford, which 'hazardous in winter and in floods, prevents many parishoners attending Divine Service and clergymen cannot attend to their duties in half of the parish over the river'. It cost £3,140.

In 1812 Mr Wood, Presbyterian minister at Falstone, decided to clear a site at Hawkhope where Armstrong marks ruins, It was probably the site of an old chapel, and he unearthed the famous Falstone stone. It was part of the socket of a cross and carried the earliest post-Roman inscription in Northumberland. In modern English it reads — Eomaer set this up for his uncle Hroethberht. Pray for his soul. Strictly speaking it is not from Falstone, which means 'speckled stone', nor does it refer to Robsons, one of the old families of the area. The chapel at Fourstones is mentioned in 1541, but it seems to have been neglected, and in 1715 the ruins are said to have been rebuilt and used by the Presbyterians, who were very strong in numbers in this part. An Anglican chapel was built in 1725, but it was not well attended.

10. Falstone Road Bridge.

After 1814 Falstone became a separate parish and by 1824 Greenwich Hospital, the owners of the land since Derwentwater's rebellion, built a new church and rectory, in a special style as at Greystead, Wark and Thorneyburn. The rectors were retired naval chaplains and seem to have found life in these remote parts very different. In 1832 Revd. Mr Burdon had become 'restless, expensive, drunken, embarrassed and eventually insane in retirement'. The church was burned in 1890 and was rebuilt in much the same style. A number of fragments of Anglican crosses have been found in this area. The churchyard is remarkable for the number of gravestones, some of them very curiously carved with figures. One is called the 'Dance of Death', and others show the strange skill of an unknown sculptor.

There were no Catholics or Methodists in Falstone at this time, but Oliver wrote.

Ministers in communion with the Church of Scotland, were assiduously employed in imparting religious instruction to the neglected people of this part of the country long before the Church of England thought them worthy of attention: and the consequence is, that the Presbyterian Chapel at Falstone is every Sunday, crowded, while that of the Church of England is comparatively empty.

The Presbyterian attendance included dogs as well as people. The shepherds brought their dogs with them, and they were well behaved until the congregation rose for the final blessing. The dogs rising caused pandemonium, and so in future people were to remain seated for the blessing. (1819). The Presbyterian congregation of Falstone with Kielder numbered something like 1,000 at this time.

The original Presbyterian Chapel at Falstone, dated 1709, was re-built in

24

1807, and again rebuilt with a tower in 1876. The Duke of Northumberland had
another Presbyterian Chapel built at Kielder in 1874 for his workmen and their
families.

11. Carved Gravestone in Falstone Churchyard.

Railways had increased the population and made travel easier. In North
Tyndale there were a number of old surnames of kinships, strongly supporting
their own members in feuds against the Scots and other raiders. They were the
Charltons, Robsons, Dodds. Milburns and Ridleys. So many of them might
inhabit a village like Falstone that it was difficult to distinguish them by Christian names. Newly arrived ministers or schoolmasters might be very confused.
Villagers distinguished each other by nick-names rather like the Welsh. A new
servant at the manse was a Robson, who went by the name of 'Sally the Clog-
ger'. A Mr Robson was 'laird' in the 1820's and lived at Falstone Farm, a strong
house near the church. It incorporates a 'bastle', that has a vaulted basement
with walls 3½ feet thick. The lintel above the door is embodied within the
farmhouse and carries the letters A B C D E F G 1604 H I K . This is curious
since initials usually indicate a marriage with the new couple taking over the
house. The south front of the house was remodelled in the seventeenth century.
There is another bastle at Hawkhope, not vaulted, but with walls 4 feet thick.
At Ridge End, where the Smalesburn joins the North Tyne, is yet another
bastle. There are many in this area: the old cottages were low and thatched with
turf and heather.

The inn at Falstone is called the Black Cock. It was there in the 1820s serving anglers, shooters and walkers, and is still there. The black cock was the moorland grouse, preserved by the landowners. In 1834 they formed the North Tyne and Redewater Association for the Prevention of Poaching. It was difficult for those who inherited the blood of the reivers, and both Oliver (1835) and Palmer (1888) indicate that poaching still went on.

Thorneyburn

Following a narrow road north of the river, Donkleywood is reached, where there are the ruins of a bastle with walls 5 feet thick. Next comes Thorneyburn overlooking the river. In 1818 the Commissioners of Greenwich Hospital intended to build a church here, but failed to secure the land. They acquired land further up the Tarset Burn at Drapercroft, but since Thorneyburn was in the contract, Thorneyburn Church is here, two miles from Thorneyburn and the old station.

Archdeacon Singleton paid a visit in 1832 and found a fine church and new rectory with gardens, but the rector and his wife.

"Having passed most of their lives at Portsmouth and Plymouth (when he was naval chaplain) seem but little satisfied with the absolute seclusion. They are moreover surrounded by waters, the Tarset with its steep and precipitous banks is to be forded towards the north and the rapid Tyne is to be traversed to the south. I came to Thorneyburn in a four wheeled carriage from Elsdon by High Green and the fearful descent of the Gate House and the Ford of the Tarset, and left it by crossing the Tyne at a ford a little below Greystead on my way to Bellingham". Bellingham bridge not built until 1834.

Meanwhile the curate at Falstone, Mr Kennedy, had kept a kind of diary on the shutters of the rectory, and often the sad comment on his life was the word 'solus' meaning alone. These parts could be very lonely to those not used to the kind of life and not involved in work by farm, field or quarry.

Having crossed the river to Greystead, another Greenwich Hospital Church, Archdeacon Singleton wrote of his visit.

This is the poorest and most secluded of all the new rectories...the smartness of the place has gone, as the Revd. M. Rennell the Rector is in confinement as a lunatic at Newcastle, and Mr Stubbs, the curate, a respectable non-graduate has no means of keeping up the neatness of the walks and fences and shrubberies.

He added later.

I almost suspect that the contrast from the din and bustle of the wardroom and cockpit school of a man of war to the stillness and solitude of these moorland benefices is too great for those who do not seek refuge in literature of some sort or another.

Mr Wallis of Simonburn had occupied himself with compiling his *Natural History of Northumberland*.

Today Thorneyburn still seems remote. Trees have grown up to shelter the rectory and the church. The walls and trees are covered with mosses and lichens. The daffodils follow the snowdrops and the swallows come back in the summer. The school has been closed and the children go to Greenhaugh. The church was threatened with redundancy by the Church Commissioners and this provoked an immediate response from the neighbourhood. Money has been raised, repairs effected and the interior beautifully re-decorated in such a way as to show the classical contours and style of the church, with no division of nave and chancel. It has a fine stained glass window at the east end and an absence of any fussy decoration. The Greenwich Hospital churches are unusual in style for Northumberland, and built at a time when few Anglican churches were being built. Apart from Falstone they have not suffered from Victorian restoration.

Bastles

12. **Redheugh Farmhouse on the Tarset Burn.**

The Tarset valley had a number of bastle houses. On the eastern side there are two at Gatehouse, and further north there is one at Black Middens. This is now an ancient monument in the care of English Heritage and can be visited. It is well built of fairly large stones. Better squared stones are used for the corners, but rough coursed between. The original entrance was in the east end at ground level and rather narrow. The entrance to the upper floor is now reached by stone steps. This floor was timbered, with stone at the west end for the hearth. The building is now roofless and some stumps of old beams can be seen. There are ruins of other buildings to the east. A mile further north across the Tarset Burn is Corbie Castle. This stands a single storey high, and the vaulted basement has partly collapsed. On the same side of the stream further south is a farm called Redheugh, which has a date-stone W C 1732, but this is the date of re-construction of the old bastle. Further south on Shilla Hill is another bastle, in ruinous condition, and finally at Camp Cottage, a farm house on a low hill overlooking the Tyne are the remains of another ruinous building of the bastle type.

The Tarset Burn is attractive in a wild way, with its windings and waterfalls. It was well known for salmon, and in 1920 Anderson Graham walking there met a countryman:

There is a twinkle in his eye as he suggests that is is a fine sight, and a leading question or two brings out the fact that the deadly poaching instrument, the cleek, is not unknown in these solitudes. On one occasion, in fact, he took 45 large salmon from this burn...and he pointed out that the first salmon to go up these burns are fair game. The floods which enable the earlier fish to ascend do not last long and in the end fish are marooned in pools. So you might as well have them.

Tarset Castle

The stream passes the northern scarp of Tarset Castle and underneath a three-arched railway bridge to join the North Tyne. The Chirdon Burn comes in from the west, so here is a meeting of the waters. The valley becomes wider with lush meadows on either side, but crossing the waters of Tyne was always a problem till the modern bridges were built. This was an area where there were larger defensive buildings — Tarset Castle and Dally Castle, both going back to the thirteenth century and now completely in ruins.

In 1267/68 John Comyn was granted a licence by Henry III to crenellate (i.e. fortify) a hall which he proposed to build at Tarset. His son, Red Comyn, was later murdered by Robert Bruce. The castle was defended by a stone wall and a ditch. It was on a site of great strategic importance, commanding the fords of Tyne and Tarset, and also two traffic routes — one from Housesteads to Dere Street and the other from Deadwater to Hexham. It had a turbulent history, and in 1523 it was occupied by Sir Ralph Fenwick and 80 men. They were attacked by Willian Charlton of Bellingham with 200 men and driven out (1524). In 1525 Fenwick returned with 100 men to hold the castle. This time the castle was taken by an unholy alliance of Tynedale men and Scots, who destroyed it by fire. It was never restored, and was used as a quarry to build a neighbouring farmhouse and field walls. In 1888 it was excavated and a stone underground passage discovered, probably a sewer. But the stone was taken away. The railway cut across the western side of the castle area. There are still remains on top of the mound, and the castle seems to have been a rectangular building like Haughton with corner towers, surrounded by a stone wall and outer ditch. Prolonged excavation would be necessary to obtain a complete plan, but it is a fine vantage point for surveying the North Tyne with Dally and Hesleyside on the other side of the valley.

Dally Castle

Dally is approached by a narrow road along the Chirdon Burn, now leading into a Forestry area. There is a mill, a farm, cottages and the ruined castle. It was first mentioned in the thirteenth century and consisted of a rectangular building defended by loopholes. Later the building was heightened and two turrets added with battlements, so the loopholes were filled in and the walls strengthened. It was ruinous by the reign of Janes I, and stone was removed to build Dally Mill and other premises. Some fine columns that had supported the hall roof were taken away to build pigsties.

The castle stood at the end of a ridge, overlooking the ford, where later a packhorse or footbridge was built.

The valley of the Chirdon Burn is very attractive, lined with ancient alders, contorted by age and wind, and encrusted with mosses and lichens. In the gloom they could look like spectral figures. We were told of one man, who 'nicked' a fine salmon, thought he was being watched and dived into a ditch where he hid for some time, cold and wet. He got out to give himself up and found that the 'observer' was nothing but an old alder tree!

13. Greystead Church, built by Greenwich Hospital.

Greystead

Returning to what was the main road before the Kielder Reservoir, we cross the vocal Chirdon Burn by a hump backed bridge at right angles to the road, which then winds and undulates on its unpredictable way towards Bellingham. The North Tyne Valley is now much more widespread, but there are heights at a distance on either side. After passing the Moorcock, another old inn, we come to Greystead, another of the Greenwich Hospital Churches. The architect was H. H. Seward, who was a pupil of Sir John Soane. Pevsner wrote —

A sister church of those at Humshaugh, Wark and Thorneyburn. The same window tracery, the same pretty internal proportions. The W. tower, however, has the distinguishing motif of a group of three lancet bell openings.

It is well situated with a fine view over the Tyne Valley, and there are very attractive mature trees. In 1922 Greystead was combined with Thorneyburn. A hundred years earlier when both churches were built, it had been proposed that one church should be built and a bridge to enable those from the other side to attend. The cost of two churches and two rectories (1818) was £17,000.

29

Hesleyside

The road continues through beautifully wooded country to Hesleyside. Hodgson wrote — *It stands on a gentle eminence: the grounds around it are well clothed with wood and agreeable diversified by fine sheep walks.* (1813). It has been associated for centuries with the Charlton family and neighbouring Charlton, which once had a tower, belonged to them as well as other places. Familiar is the sixteenth century image of them as depicted by Bell Scott on one of the Wallington murals. The men are assembled on either side of a long table, looking ravenously hungry. The lady of the house has come in with a large covered dish and lifting the cover shows nothing but a spur. The message was plain — if you want food, ride and get some! This was the practice of the reivers, and at the time of Lent food would be naturally short in those days.

At Hesleyside a house and tower were mentioned in 1537, and in 1541 it was reported that since the destruction of Tarset Castle, there were no other towers standing in Tynedale but Hesleyside. In the seventeenth century, as at other places such as Chipchase, a wing was added and there was a date 1631 on some of the old stonework. The original tower stood to the west of this structure and was pulled down during later developments. In 1719 the hall was constructed with a new south-facing facade. A secret chamber was preserved — this was the priest's hide. The Charltons were Catholics and continued to keep the old faith despite penalising legislation.

In 1738 the Hall suffered severely from fire, and during a prolonged period of rebuilding there were two more damaging fires. From 1796 William Newton

14. Hesleyside Hall, home of the Charltons.

rebuilt the old south-facing wing and added another in different style to the east, so that Hesleyside finally emerges as ranges of buildings about an open courtyard, quadrangular in plan. The east wing is 3 storeys high and 7 windows wide. The south front is of the same height with 11 windows width. Entrance is by a central archway and above it an ornamental shield, set out from the wall, ventilates the secret chamber.

The old formal gardens were destroyed and new gardens were laid out. Pevsner says that Capability Brown was responsible for changes from 1776 and his original plans are still at the house. The little stream was used in the landscaping and parkland trees were set. There is a fine view from the east front to the river and conversely, from the river, the house is framed by avenues of trees, a very attractive setting.

Bellingham

We move along the river towards Bellingham and cross by that important bridge of 1834, which abolished the fitful practice of fording. In 1760 Bishop Pococke had written *There is not one bridge over the North Tyne, but they have a summer ford at the town and a winter ford a mile lower called Bridge Ford.* In 1824 the governors of Greenwich Hospital obtained an act for opening up their property by roads and bridges. It included a road from Hexham by Simonburn to Bellingham. John Green, favourite architect of the Duke of Northumberland, designed the Bellingham bridge which made the necessary link across the waters. It has four arches and it seems that the old toll house is still standing.

Bellingham could be described as the capital of North Tynedale — the only settlement of more than a thousand people in a very large area. In the sixteenth century and after, it was the centre for the sale of food products. It was obviously very much involved in Border warfare and the activities of the moss troopers. The local men could retreat into steep valleys where fallen trees and bogs prevented pursuit. There were many timber defence works, and a scarcity of castles and large houses. Houses of ordinary people were stone built, low and thatched with heather and turf. There was a market for sheep and cattle with two annual fairs in March and September. Bellingham Fair still continues, and when the railways ran, it was a particularly great occasion. *The wool fair of Bellingham is one of the largest in the county. The Saturday following September 15th is the date of 'Cuddy's Fair' (St. Cuthbert's). When the old custom is observed of 'riding the fair', at the conclusion of which the charter is read. Muggers' Hill has received its name from the muggers or potters who attend the fairs and always select the ground for the display of their wares. The river is crossed by a picturesque bridge, built in 1835. Hotels and Inns — Railway Hotel, Black Bull, Fox and Hounds, Rose and Crown, Temperance Hotel,* (Tomlinson 1888).

He adds that Muckle Jock of Bellingham more than once cleared the fair with the Tarset and Tarret men at his back, shouting the old Border cry —

> *Tarset and Tarret burn,*
> *Hard and heather bred*
> *Yet — yet — yet.*

Yet is the local pronunciation of gate, and it means clear the way or get out of the way. It echoes back to mediaeval times.

31

Bellingham was a chapelry of Simonburn, a huge parish stretching from the Roman Wall to the Scottish Border. Priests were not too willing to serve in these remote and dangerous areas. The Church of St. Cuthbert stands on an eminence overlooking the river. Reginald of Durham recorded that St. Cuthbert performed a miracle here, and the quaint water pant down the back lane from the church and still flowing, is called St. Cuthbert's Well.

The church has a long history; dowsing indicates that there were two timber structures before the first stone built church. This was demolished in the late twelfth century, and another church was built with aisle-less chancel and a nave of four bays with narrow aisles. A transept was added on the south side, divided into two chapels. With the Scottish Wars and local poverty there came a period of long neglect. but in the seventeenth century, by the efforts of Cuthbert Ridley, rector of Simonburn, it was rebuilt. The choir was restored, the aisles were demolished and the nave rebuilt with thick walls covering the old pillars. The walls had to carry a heavy load, a barrel vaulted roof of stone, supported by ribs. This was in the Scottish style and Scottish connections have been suggested. A roof of this kind was fire-proof. In the eighteenth century the windows were altered and buttresses added to support the walls. Further improvements were made in the nineteenth century, when the choir was re-roofed. Damp was a problem since earth around the outside of the church had risen to a height of 5 feet, above the nave floor.

There are a number of medieval grave slabs, and one of the north of the church has been associated with the story of the 'Long Pack'. It might be briefly told as follows:

About 1732 a pedlar called at Lee Hall, the home of Colonel Ridley. None of the family was at home and a girl who was there gave the pedlar permission to leave his long pack in the hall, while he went elsewhere. Later the girl thought she saw the pack move and called in the house boy and an old servant. The boy, also thinking he saw the pack move, fired at it with a gun. There was a great groan and blood flowed from the pack. Undoing the wrappings they found an armed man inside with a whistle round his neck. They called in neighbours to help, and later at night when then whistle was blown a gang of robbers attacked. They were met with a hail of gunfire, and finally made off with the wounded (and dead). The dead man inside was never identified nor claimed for burial, but it has provided a popular story.

Hareshaw Ironworks

Bellingham is quite a pleasant place with several inns and cafes to cater for tourists or travellers along the Pennine Way. It is good for walkers with moorland and forest. A particularly attractive area is Hareshaw Lynn, a local waterfall. Here at one time was an industrial centre — the Hareshaw Ironworks. The Duke of Northumberland had given his approval to mining of the ironstone and coal on Hareshaw Common. The works were built in 1838 and leased to Messrs. Batson, Campion & Co. There were two furnaces — later three — and power from a waterwheel and steam engine. A waggonway connected the ironworks with the Hareshaw collieries; waste heaps can still be seen. Coke ovens roasted the coal for making coke. Six rows of cottages were provided for

Simonburn

Eventually we reach Simonburn, where once was a Saxon church as indicated by a number of carved stones. After the Norman Conquest the advowson of the church belonged to the King of Scotland. His lands were taken over by Edward I, and he presented priests to the church, but the Bishop of Durham made a counter claim. In 1490 Bishop Fox ordered that the Rector of Simonburn should have a tower for his safety, since the church was some distance from the castle. In the survey of 1541 it was reported that at Simonburn the rectory was 'a little tower in fairly good repair'.

It was difficult to get suitable ministers who would stay. In 1595 Lord Eure, Lord Warden of the Marches asked for the right to present his candidate *Mr Crakenthorp, Master of Arts of Oxenforde...and is a devoute godlie and learned man...my son's tutor.* But Mr Crakenthorp refused the living *deaminge his body unable to live in so troublesome a place & his nature not well brooking the perverse nature of so crooked a people.*

Dowsing would seem to indicate that there was a church or churches existing before any of the stonework standing — the west wall and the chancel arch dating back to the thirteenth century. The dedication of the church is to St. Mungo or Kentigern. It is claimed that St. Mungo's Well was on the site. The pillars of the arches are thirteenth century, indicating that there could be a church without aisles in an earlier period. It seems that the church was not well maintained, the rectors being absentees and duties being done by curates, if available. In 1290 the son of the Earl of Gloucester was appointed Rector; he

16. Simonburn Church.

held 29 preferments in 14 dioceses, and so was not likely to pay much attention to Simonburn. Other Rectors were absentees, and by 1604 the churches of the parish were in ruins. In that year Cuthbert Ridley, member of a local family, became Rector and devoted himself to restoring the churches. He rebuilt Bellingham and restored Simonburn, including the south chapel which became the family chapel. Here are still the figures from a monument — himself, wife and two children. He died in 1636. "In the Day of Judgement God be merciful to Ridley a sinner'.

Another good rector was Henry Wastell (1723 - 1771) who carried out further repairs, and rebuilt the rectory. He also paid a shepherd to collect inscribed stones from the Roman Wall when it was being demolished to make the Military Road. Simonburn is hardly four miles from the Roman Wall and Roman stone could have been used in building the medieval church. Robert Newton and his son William, of Newcastle were responsible for the repairs and improvements to the church, including new windows. Wastell encouraged his curate, Wallis to write his *Natural History of Northumberland.*

In 1771 came Dr. James Scott (a political appointment) who soon offended Wallis. He also enraged his parishioners by his excessive demands for tithes. An attempt was made on his life, and so he decided to leave the area for London. In 1809 he allowed the church to be stripped of its lead roofing 'for war purposes' and the new covering was slates.

In 1863 when the choir was extensively rebuilt, much of the old masonry was used, rehewn. A few years later the nave was rebuilt, so that the church looked very different from the old pictures of it. It also differs greatly from the Greenwich Hospital collection of churches, which came with the division of the parish.

The Crook or Tecket burn comes into Simonburn from the west and passes under two low arched bridges. The burn makes an attractive valley, and its waters can be traced back to Tecket Lynn, where a gorge with gigantic rocks cause the waters to come rushing down in cascades. The valley has steep sides and is attractively wooded, providing haunts for ousels and rooks. The trees are covered with moss and lichen. In a cave or grotto near the waterfalls, John Wallis worked on his book, away from the clamour and dogs of the rectory.

Along the Castle burn, near its junction with the Hopeshiel burn, stand the ruins of Simonburn Castle in a strong position. It was listed in 1415 and 1541, it was in good repair, recommended as suitable for a garrison of 100 men under the keeper, to take the place of Tarset, which had been destroyed. Its ruin was helped by the activities of unofficial treasure seekers. In the eighteenth century it was purchased by the Allgoods of Nunwick, and it was repaired as a folly or 'eye-catcher'. Since that time ruin has come again, and trees have encroached on the walls. The face of the tower, the part still standing measures 35 feet across, and a turret projected 8 feet on the north west side. The basement of the tower was tunnel vaulted with walls about 5 feet in thickness on either side of the 16 feet vault. Other details are difficult to trace. It once commanded extensive views over valley and hill. The woodland here is picturesque, and it makes a pleasant walk from Simonburn, an estate type village about a green. The cot-

quarries and the great road vehicles grinding away with their burdens. Meanwhile the Swin Burn gurgles and grouses its way down to Barrasford and empties into the North Tyne near the old mill.

Here there used to be a ferry to Haughton Castle across the river; this is one of the finest views on the North Tyne. Having crossed the dismantled railway by bridge, we make our way along the east bank of the river to Chollerton.

19. North Tyne near Chollerford.

Chollerton

Chollerton was a manor of the barony of Prudhoe and held by the Swin-burns. Since they also held Haughton, a medieval ferry was maintained. The Erring Burn comes into the North Tyne below Chollerton, from which place can be seen the river, Cocklaw Tower and the line of the Roman Wall. The Church at Chollerton is very unusual — a passing glance conveys the impression 'restored in the 19th century', but there is very much more than this. Dowsing had indicated that there was a Saxon church here, but the earliest stonework is of the Norman period at the west end and at the base of the chancel arch. It was aisle-less and then a south aisle was added; the pillars supporting the arches were Roman columns taken from the fort at Chesters. A Roman altar was also used as a font. Later, in medieval times, a north aisle was added. The chancel is difficult to date since it was very much restored in the eighteenth century. The tower at the west end was added about 1769, and this was adorned with a wooden spire a century later. There are a number of medieval grave covers and carved stones. In the churchyard among a number of interesting monuments is one to members of the family of Saint, who were millers at a fulling mill on the Erring Burn. A mill is carved at the top of the grave slab. Near the church is a farm that had a windmill and a steam engine at different times with different

43

power. There is a building near the church that was used as a stable for members of the congregation travelling from a distance by horse. The station is used now as a house, and the road below passes under a remarkably skewed railway bridge. It is hoped that this will be preserved as an excellent piece of railway architecture. The Redesmouth viaduct has been demolished. The road here is known as the Alemouth or Corn Road, which was built in the middle of the eighteenth century to convey produce from central Northumberland to the coast. The Military Road, which crosses it some two miles further on, was built at the same time. Previously roads had often been impassable because of lack of maintenance. There is much evidence of stone quarrying about — used for housing, farm buildings and walls. Limestone was also burnt for agricultural purposes, and the massive lime kilns on the railway near Cocklaw should also be preserved as industrial monuments.

20. Chollerton Church Stable.

Over the fields can be seen the stonework of Cocklaw Tower; this stone was quarried by the Romans to construct Hadrian's Wall, and was later looted by medieval castle builders. It was better to use ready cut stone rather than quarry it. The Military Road finished off the Roman Wall for many miles, since it was used for road foundations. South of Cocklaw on the ridge that carries the Roman wall is the little church of St. Oswald. It is partly built of Roman stone and there is a Roman altar inside. The Battle of Heavenfield was fought here in 634 A.D., when Oswald, King of Northumbria, erected a wooden cross in a prepared position and fought in the name of Jesus Christ against Cadwallon and his pagan army. He won a great victory, and another wooden cross to-day marks the site of the battle. From St. Oswald's Chapel on the Wall, magnificent views extend, including the wanderings of the North Tyne.

Cocklaw tower below is a substantial structure, very like Chipchase and measuring 50½ feet by 34½ feet with thick walls. It looks smaller because the bartizans or corner towers and the battlements have fallen. It has a vaulted basement, which is still used for farm purposes, but the floors above have fallen to time and decay. In the last century, when the interior was in better condition, parts of the walls retained medieval painting, indicating that these places were not so grim as might appear today. There were small windows at the higher level and only a loophole in the basement. A spiral staircase led up to the upper storeys and the roof. The first floor was the main residential area, with a hall and private apartment called the 'painted chamber'. Beneath it, reached only from a trapdoor in the floor, is what has been called the dungeon, but it could also be regarded as a safe or secret hiding place. In the time of its military use, the tower would have a strong walled enclosure. There is now only the farmyard enclosing wall, like a field wall.

21. Cocklaw Tower.

Below Cocklaw the road is very close to the river and crosses the railway by a stone bridge. The railway, partly overgrown, provides a winter shelter for the cattle. A farm on the road is called Dunkirk, not after the events of 1940, but after a victory of Oliver Cromwell in the Low Countries over the Spaniards. Dunkirk was captured from the enemy and replaced Calais that had been lost by Queen Mary in 1558. Charles II rather foolishly sold Dunkirk to the French, and it was used by privateers to prey on English shipping in the Channel.

Chollerford

The Corn Road meets the Military Road and a right turn leads to the bridge at Chollerford, rebuilt in 1775, after the Great Tyne Flood of 1771 demolished all the bridges except the one at Corbridge. Chollerford Bridge is a very fine five-arched structure, but nowadays limited to single line traffic. The George Hotel is a hostelry that has been known for centuries and well patronised.

22. Chollerford Bridge over the North Tyne.

Humshaugh

The road to the right leads to Humshaugh, a pleasant village that has increased its population in modern times, unlike many of the North Tyne villages. It still retains its school, and there is a very fine eighteenth century house in brick, rather unusual in these parts. Humshaugh was part of the Simonburn parish, but in 1832 became a separate vicarage. A new church was built here in 1818, dedicated to St. Peter. It is another of the Greenwich Hospital style. The architect is not certainly known, but it may be John Dobson. Greenwich Hospital had the patronage, and during the nineteenth century ex-naval chaplains were appointed. Humshaugh is not nearly so remote as some of the other churches.

A narrow road continues towards Haughton, where once was a village. It was removed to enlarge the parkland, but part if the medieval chapel was retained as a landscape feature.

Haughton Castle

The castle of Haughton, overlooking the North Tyne, is another of great importance, picturesque in its setting and appealing to romantic travellers and painters as well as architectural historians. At first here was a mansion or country house and unfortified. It may have been single storeyed and then another level added. For some time it was held by Swinburns, but after Adam Swinburn died c. 1317 his lands were divided between his three daughters. Gerald Widdrington, who married one of them gained Haughton. He owned Widdrington Castle and was responsible for converting Haughton from a 'hall house' into a castle. He built up the arched recesses that can be seen in the walls, making them very strong. The building was heightened so that the great hall could be on the second floor. Additional apartments were a private room or solar

46

and a chapel. There were turrets at each corner with a spiral stair in the S. E. one. The basement was vaulted and the building had been made into a strong fortress.

The Widdringtons, however, preferred to live at Widdrington Castle and Haughton was somewhst neglected suffering from Scottish attacks. In 1541 Armstrongs, Elliots and Crosiers attacked it and by scaling ladders broke in. They injured the keeper, took nine horses and goods worth £40.

23. Haughton Castle.

At Haughton 2 myles southeste from the said town of Symondburne standeth the walles of an olde castell or fortress very stronge but ye roofes and floores thereof bene decayed and gone. And an old barmekyn partly decayed in the walles thereof of thinherytaunce of Sir John Wetherington knighte and in greatt decaye.

A family called Smith from Teckett lived only in part of it, yet later one of them, William Smith, a sea captain (1751 - 1825), was to restore it. He was called 'the Buccaneer', and no doubt became wealthy from his maritime adventures. The main entrance of the castle was moved to the north front. The park was enclosed and the road diverted; the old village was removed and a walled garden was established.

In 1788 William Smith opened a water powered paper mill on the river below the castle. It prospered and he manufactured special paper, which was literally

47

used for making money i.e. paper currency. When war developed between Britain and Revolutionary France the paper was used to forge French paper money called 'assignats'. This was taken into the Low Countries with the purpose of undermining the French financial system. The notes were manufactured at Haughton. William Smith also offered his castle for use as an arms store against possible French invasion. Haughton Mill had ceased working by 1888. by this time Haughton Castle had been purchased by Mr Cruddas, and he was responsible for further reconstruction and improvements. Pevsner comments on the building. *The aesthetic delight in this fine tall, symetrically grouped front is matched by the archaeological interest of the building history and the details.* The castle contains some fine artistic treasures, including two large carved Jacobean overmantels from Derwentwater House, Newcastle.

24. North Tyne near Haughton.

Chesters

The North Tyne flows under Chollerford Bridge, past the mill to Chesters, important as a Roman site and country house. It is an interesting diversion to cross the bridge and follow the course of the river by a field path. Eventually the line of the Roman Wall is reached; Hadrian's Wall was the official frontier for centuries. Here is the abutment for a bridge that carried the wall and a road over the river to Chesters fort. The bridge has gone and the waters flow deep, so that you have to go to the official entrance on the other side of the river. The country house which takes its name from the Roman 'castrum' or fort is not open to the public, but can be seen from the Roman fort in the parkland below it.

Chesters owes a great deal to the Clayton family. The original house was built about 1771 for the Erringtons. The architect was John Carr of York. In 1796 the house was sold to Nathaniel Clayton of Newcastle, who was Town Clerk for 37 years from 1785. Chesters was his country house, and he died there in 1832. In 1822, when he retired as Town Clerk, he was succeeded by his son, John Clayton (born 1792). John was a classical scholar, lawyer, town planner and

48

archaeologist, living to the remarkable (at that time) age of 98. During that period he left his impression on town and country, land and water. He was intimately concerned with the Newcastle and Carlisle Railway — the project was strongly opposed, and he was much involved in the legal battles and getting a Bill through Parliament. He had to defend Newcastle during the Municipal Reform period from 1834. When the Tyne Conservancy Board was established, it was his duty to look after Newcastle's interests. In 1850 he became clerk to the Tyne Conservancy Commissioners. During this period too he was involved with Dobson and Grainger in the redevelopment of Newcastle. They could not have managed the business without him, and it is quite amazing to consider the amount of work he undertook. In 1867 he decided to resign and could not be persuaded to stay on. He was never idle, and was able to devote his time to other activities including the development of his estate.

25. Roman Baths at Chesters.

He was a very active antiquary, and like his father a member of the Newcastle Society of Antiquaries. His great desire was to preserve the Roman Wall, and whenever lands carrying the Wall came on to the market, he purchased them — Carrawburgh, Chesterholm and Housesteads included. He was involved in excavations at Chesters and elsewhere, reported in *Archaeologia Aeliana*. Collingwood Bruce was his friend and they worked together on the Wall. Clayton built a museum at Chesters to house his fine collection of Roman Antiquities. He was specially interested in Roman inscriptions. His collection is still on view to those who visit the Roman fort, now in the care of English Heritage.

Clayton died in 1890 and was succeeded by his nephew at Chesters, Nathaniel George, son of his brother the Revd. Richard Clayton. There is a monument to Nathaniel George Clayton (1833 - 1895) and his wife in Humshaugh Church.

John Clayton did a great deal for Humshaugh too — the church, school, reading room and Library. The range of his achievements is quite remarkable. Chesters is perhaps the most delightful of the Roman forts to visit. Hodgson

49

wrote — *Since the Claytons settled here, they have seen all their own and neigh-bouring grounds and distant brown and naked heights sheltered and beautified with thriving plantations of pine and great varieties of deciduous trees and the meadows of Chesters become the emerald area of a very rich and picturesque amphitheatre.*

The pasture land is valuable and so only part of the fort has been exposed by excavation - all the gateways with their guard houses, part of the barrack blocks, the foundations of the headquarters with strong room and the commandant's house. At least half the fort stood out beyond the Wall, so that the Roman forces could easily get out to attack the enemy. On a lower level, outside the fort, but behind the Wall was the bath house. This is the best example on Hadrian's Wall, and the visitor can look at the changing room, the hot, cold and warm baths and the heating system. One can see where the Roman bridge went across the North Tyne. There was also a vicus or civilian settlement behind the Wall and out-side the fort. Much of this is explained by the plans, photographs and exhibits in the museum.

The Roman soldiers were not men from sunny Italy, cowering in the cold against wind that blew round their naked legs and sandalled feet. Coming from all parts of the Roman Empire, they lived in stone barrack blocks, and the fort was surrounded by a 20 foot wall. There was under-floor heating in some parts and heating in the baths, which was the social centre. Chesters was not a bad place at which to be stationed, and there was good hunting and fishing to be enjoyed. Moreover the Roman troops were well fed, and each fort had supplies for one year. At one time the soldiers at Chesters were Asturians from Northern Spain. Troops served at various different stations in their time. Fresh water was always brought down to the fort from higher ground, and ended by flushing the latrines at the lowest level.

Hodgson, again an enthusiast for Rome wrote of *the steep and woody banks of the North Tyne where it sometimes lingers in its course to admire the hawthorn bowers of Chesters and then with a sort of arrowy speed, dashes its dark coloured waters through a narrow and rocky sided channel, past Walwick Grange and the Mills of Wall and Warden, to its nuptials with the South Tyne, near Hexham.*

The Romans depicted the river Tyne as a god, as in Chesters Museum. We know that Roman boats were able to reach Corbridge, but could they ever nav-igate the North Tyne, which was a very different proposition? They might have reached Chesters, but further would have been very difficult, and the Romans had good roads and road transport.

Watersmeet at Warden

The North and South Tyne actually meet near the village of Warden. There is a pleasant walk from the Boat Inn along the bank of the South Tyne to the meeting of the waters. The Boat Inn was formerly the place of a ferry until the toll bridge was built across the river. The toll house still stands, but the old bridge was replaced in 1904 by a County structure. The Newcastle — Carlisle Railway crosses the river by a strongly built iron bridge, and in the distance can be seen the Church of St John Lee on high ground. The Corn Road and the Border Railway approach Hexham on the other side of the river through the village of Wall.

26. Warden Church with Lychgate.

Warden is an interesting village: it is dominated by the old motte, now tree covered, and higher still are the earthworks of a prehistoric fort. The church at Warden is dedicated to St Michael, and has a fine upstanding Anglo Saxon tower dating back to the eleventh century, and built of Roman stone. Indications are that there was a church earlier than the tower, and in the post Conquest period, another church was added to the tower. The tower arch is built of Roman material, probably from Chesters. Transepts were added in the thirteenth century making the church cruciform in shape. There were alterations in the eighteenth century, and the chancel was rebuilt in 1889. There are a number of incised grave covers in the porch, and a carved piece of stone which looks as if it may be Roman. Warden is situated on a triangle of land between the two Tynes. It had a water mill on the North Tyne and a paper mill on the South Tyne, which started in 1763 and still exists. A century ago a visitor described how the rags were converted into beautiful white paper. The mill employed 63 hands. He was not impressed by the Methodist Church built in 1851.

In appearance it resembles a barn rather than an ecclesiastical edifice. and he hoped it might soon be rebuilt. No doubt he had in mind Warden Church and the Revd. Canon Cruddas. Another report was —

At West Boat there was an elegant suspension bridge which was erected in 1826 at a cost of £5,000. In 1877 it gave way beneath the weight of a steam thresher which was passing over. It was repaired and later replaced by the stone bridge which crosses the South Tyne to the Hexham road.

There is said to be a ghost at Warden in what is called Homer's Lane, the scene of an unsolved murder mystery — that of Joe the Quilter, whose work graced many of Northumberland bed. He was last seen (1900) by a housemaid returning to Chesters from a dance, whether him or his ghost. He lived near here, and his ghost is said to be one-legged, since he had lost one of his clogs in a frantic effort to escape his murderer. So do not walk this way alone on a dark night!

It is now time to trace the course of the South Tyne to its place of meeting with the North Tyne. Thinking of Hodgson's 'nuptials', can we regard the rivers as feminine and masculine respectively? North Tyne seems noisier and tougher.

27. Roman Water Nymphs in Chesters Museum.

Chapter Three
THE SOUTH TYNE

In searching for sources of the South Tyne, the place to visit is Cross Fell. It stands 2,930 feet above sea level, and has an annual rainfall of 70 inches. In fine weather it provides a marvellous viewpoint over several counties — Yorkshire, Durham, Cumbria and Northumberland. Westwards can be seen lakes, mountains and the Solway, and immediately there is a steep fall of 2,000 feet towards the River Eden. A remarkable feature of Cross Fell is the appearance of the Helm wind, which causes great turbulence on the treeless upper slopes. It gets its name from a cloud that hangs 'like a helmet'.

There is *a sudden hurricane of which warning is given by a long ridge of cloud along the escarpment, with a dark layer over the valley proper, especially powerful in the late spring or autumn and viciously cold.* An investigating scientist found his hut walls (for shelter was much needed) coated with ice. The wind is very bad for hill farmers, affecting both crops and lambs.

Cross Fell was once known as Fiends' Fell, inhabited by howling demons, but these were driven out by St Augustine, who set up a Christian cross, and so the name of the fell was changed.

People, however, have come and camped at a height in order to witness dawn or sunset. The terrain is difficult, being limestone, and there are curious holes and gullies. Water can disappear underground to emerge miles away. The Pennine Way comes from the South, and a weary traveller comes down to Garrigill for a drink. There is also a Roman Road called Maiden Way, which comes from the South towards Whitley Castle.

It is noticeable in this area that on the Cumbrian side streams are called 'becks', whereas on the Northumberland side we have 'burns'. Becks join the River Tees, but some are called 'sikes'. The South Tyne is formed by small streams flowing southwards to Tynehead.

Farming in this area was marginal and large expanses were only rough grazing in the summertime, for which there were shielings or temporary huts. Lead mining was of the greatest importance, bringing wealth and prosperity. The lead mining families were part-time farmers and had small holdings — hence the divisions and field walls, which are characteristic of the area. Subsistence agriculture meant that cultivation was carried higher than might be expected, and declined with diminishing lead industry and mines.

Lead mining here dates back to Roman times, and lead mines are mentioned from 1130. Silver came from lead mining, and the King had a special interest. The miners were called the 'King's miners', and at Alston there was an early town with church and market. At more than 1,000 feet above sea level, it claims to be the highest in the country.

Hutchinson wrote of it two hundred years ago —

Alston is a small market town, meanly built, situated at the declivity of a steep hill, inhabited by miners. The fatigue of passing bad roads was in no sense alleviated by the scene which presented itself here. Pent in a narrow valley over which the mountains frowned with a melancholy sterility and nakedness: the wind tempestuous, impending clouds stretching forth a dark and disconsolate curtain over the face of the morning, rain beating vehemently against the windows, which were not able to resist the storm: a few trees standing near the inn tossed by the heavy blasts which howled down the valley: such were the objects which presented themselves to us at Alston.

Another visitor speaks favourably of the miners (lead) as opposed to colliers.

They were civil, industrous and intelligent and show by the dialect they speak, very little communication beyond their own dales. On a house to house visitation I found everything clean, whole and in its place: no trumpery little ornaments as in the collier's cottage. Where there is a picture it is that of a favourite minister such as Wesley. There are no periodicals or people's editions — they are not reckoned at all canny. The miners like everything good of its kind.

28. View of Alston Town.

Communications were difficult — upland tracks were used by 'braggers', who collected wool and by drovers, by pedlars, hucksters or packmen. Packmen could be carrying their own packs or using pack animals. Pack animals carried coal, salt and lead. The galloways in teams of 12 to 15 could carry 2 tons of lead between them. A 'bing' was about 8 cwt. Greenwich Hospital employed Macadam to make roads, and in 1834 began a main road from Hexham to Alston and Penrith.

The London Lead Company, a Quaker organisation dating from 1692, leased the Derwentwater estates and made their main centre at Nenthead where a smelt mill was set up. They had high standards of welfare, and from 1753 began to build a true mining village. Cottages built in groups of 4 took the place of the old huts. In 1825, 34 cottages were built with a shop, bath house, chapel, church and school.

In 1776, 19 mines produced ore worth £61,950. Improvements made were cast iron rails for the wagonways, and the engineer John Smeaton was employed to tunnel the Nent Force Level to Alston, a distance of 5 miles. It was lined with stone and used as an underground canal for 30 foot barges carrying ore. It was also a tourist attraction...*frequently undertaken by strangers, and not infrequently by parties of young persons resident in the neighbourhood. The old and often grotesque dresses worn on such occasions added to the mirth and cheerfulness which prevail — while the fine effect of vocal and instrumental music and the exercise of propelling the boat, add to the singular feeling which is excited by the idea of so bold an adventure'*

Thomas Sopwith, who wrote this (1833), was a mine surveyor. He explains that the tunnel was 9 feet high and 9 feet wide but larger in many places. The barge was poled along and candles provided the lights. Some of the geological scenery was fantastic. The canal helped to drain the mines, and provided a means of transport to Alston. It has now been sealed off for safety reasons, but adits can still be seen at Nenthead and Allendale.

Rise and Fall of Lead Mining

Alston has seen varying fortunes from the state of lead mining. In good years there was prosperity, but in bad years costs had to be cut and manpower reduced. In the 1830s for example some 2,000 persons left the Alston area. Then there was a recovery from 1849, and for 20 years the Alston mines reached the peak of production. From 1870 there was a decline, the result of foreign competition. In 1871 the population of Alston was 5,680 and Nenthead 1,811. Ten years later the figures were 4,621 and 1,419, a decline of about 20%. In 1882 the London Lead Company pulled out after 200 years. At Nenthead the smelter became derelict and masses of rubble are reminders of a once thriving industry. On the Killhope Fell top stood the chimney from the flue of the smelter.

In Alston the effects of the prosperous period were seen in the buildings. In 1870 the church of St Augustine was rebuilt and stands proudly with its spire above the hill market town. The market cross was also rebuilt. There was a Saturday market and numerous sheep and cattle fairs. In 1843 gas lights came to the town, and in 1857 the Town Hall was built. The cobbled street was widened — it falls steeply down the hill.

Coming of the Railways

A great boost to the area after the development of turnpike roads was the coming of the railway, important for the conveyance of heavy loads. As early as 1799 there was a mineral line from Lambley Colliery to Brampton, devised by the Earl of Carlisle. From 1835 the Newcastle to Carlisle Railway was in process of development, in which year 17 miles from Newcastle to Hexham was completed, and by 1836 extended to Haydon Bridge. From the other end the track extended from Carlisle to Greenhead, but the final link was not made till 1846. In 1841 the London Lead Company had saved £700 - £800 by use of available railways. It had a smelter at Langley and ore could be loaded at Haltwhistle to

55

rail wagons. In 1846 the Newcastle and Carlisle Railway was authorised to build a branch line from Haltwhistle to Alston. This involved a rise of 1,000 feet in some 18 miles and several viaducts. The largest at Lambley crossed the South Tyne on nine semi-circular arches, each of 59 feet span, the line being 110 feet above the river. The line was completed in 1852, and used to carry coal, lead, stone and lime. The Alston terminus had superior facilities to other stations, including an engine shed.

In 1865 a line from Hexham to Allendale was authorised and completed in 1868, but only as far as Allendale or more correctly Catton Road. It was used for all kinds of agricultural traffic and for passengers. The line was never profitable and its making was the result of the efforts of Thomas J. Bewicke, manager of the Beaumont Lead Company. Road transport was proving costly in face of foreign competition. Good coal could be brought to the Langley smelter, instead of the poor quality coal from Stubblick Colliery. There was direct contact with Tyneside. Unfortunately in the 1880s the lead industry was declining. Passenger traffic on the Allendale Branch ceased in 1930 and the line was closed in 1950. The Alston Branch, however, survived until 1st May, 1976, and the South Tyne can still be explored by rail as far as Haltwhistle. The railway keeps close to the river and uses the Tyne Gap. On either side the landscape rises steeply, and to the north is the line of the Roman Wall.

The main road was the Military Road, constructed after the Jacobite Rebellion of 1745 exposed the lamentable state of communication between the east and west of the country.

The South Tyne Valley is better observed from the railway than from the road. In 1851 a *Handbook to the Newcastle and Carlisle Railways* was published, since no such 'book for the guidance of the traveller has yet been issued from the press' and added 'with a visit to the Roman Wall'. A map shows the railway and the text covers the route with distances and places to visit by walking from the different stations. At Haltwhistle, 37 miles from Newcastle, 'We lose sight of the Tyne... He has here taken a southerly direction to his source in Cross Fell, by Alston'.

We can imagine what it was like in the great days of the steam trains, with goods and passengers being frequently carried along the lines with the sounds echoing through the valley. Children came from distant places to schools at Haydon Bridge and Hexham. There were milk trains that collected churns of milk into vans for a quick run into Newcastle. There were coal trains from numerous collieries and stone trains from the quarries. Special trains carried sheep and cattle to market. There were flat wagons, trucks, tanks and lumber wagons with their loads. Things could be distributed much more rapidly than by road, but horse vehicles were needed for immediate local distribution between station and customer. From 1840 there were already railway excursions for sight-seers, and Tomlinson in his Comprehensive Guide to Northumberland 1888 gives stations as the obvious places that travellers will be using.

Today, the traveller has to go by car and then on foot to seek the origins of the South Tyne. For a general view of the valley, one might take the way from Alston to Nenthead to get an impression of lead mining areas. We can still see scars, heaps and holes; These areas in winter time, when snow provides cover, are given to skiing. Hodgson in 1835 wrote: *The little valley of the Nent was once a fairy land and had its flowery meadows and wild shaws and bosky breays and Nentsbury for its capital, till the wealth of mining speculation began to improve and enlarge the narrow strips of enclosed land that fringed fields with the rubbish of its mines and levels and gutters at its head and sides and poison its sweet waters, with the washing ores and hushing away the soil and diluvial covering of the rocks, in prosecuting the discovery of veins.*

Hushing was a method of damming waters to collect a great quantity and then letting them out to scour the hillside. Huge rocks as well as smaller stones would be hurled down. The earth and vegetation were carried away. This accounts for the many stones on the valley floors and the gullies carved down the slopes. The landscape of lead mining has the aspect of a huge rabbit warren. Present day opencast mining is far worse, though some attempt is made to hide the rape of the earth.

Northwards from Nenthead the road leads to Coalcleugh and the lead mining areas of the West Allen. Southwards a narrow road called Dowang Hush leads to Garrigill and The South Tyne.

Garrigill

Garrigill is five miles from Alston and Tynehead is about the same distance from Garrigill. Cars can be taken a little beyond Hill House and from then on it is by foot. Alternatively, if you prefer horses, there is a riding school on the way, and on Tuesday April 18th, 1989, a lady was completing the marking out of a long bridle way from Derbyshire, to be the equestrian equivalent of the Pennine Way, which crosses Cross Fell itself — the highest point of the long journey. It is hard to imagine that in 1832, after passing of the Parliamentary Reform Bill, 50 brass bands played in triumph on top of Cross Fell, and how far afield was the music heard? Later Earl Grey's success in this matter was commemorated by a monument in Newcastle.

Palmer, exploring the South Tyne, mentions in 1875 that he set out from Garrigill on a Monday morning at the same time as the lead miners were going to work They were wearing clean smocks and carried shoulder bags with their week's provisions to carry them through to a Friday night. They stayed at what was called a 'shop', in fact a lodging place for a group of miners, where a fire was continuously kept burning. The lead miners formed a distinct community and had to travel some distance to their work. There were mines on the River Tees, about a mile beyond Tynehead. Another route by Cross Fell was called the 'Corpse Way', which is partly followed by the Pennine Way. At a time when there was no church at Garrigill, it was more convenient to carry corpses to Kirkhead in Cumbria, rather than to Alston.

Palmer confirms what Hodgson said about the effects of lead mining. He mentions how much water power was used, *and in return for such good offices the streams are made to receive the scouring of the mines, by which the fish are poisoned or scared away and to the lover of the picturesque it is not a little annoying to find the approach to one of the prettiest waterfalls encumbered by all the litter of lead washing apparatus.*

Waterfalls can be seen at Clargill opposite Tynehead, and at Ashgill, where the force falls 50 feet. At Cargill Burn mouth can be seen ruins of old mine buildings. The uplands are given to sheep and these are areas for grouse shooting. In 1819 Colonel Beaumont brought in some soldiers to try and check the poachers, but miners' knowledge of the territory, particularly underground, gave them a great advantage, and not one of them was caught. Some of the farms have strange names like Seldom Seen and Late and Soon. A big barn attached to the house, and both built strongly of stone is characteristic of this landscape. The walled enclosures are near the farm, and the open spaces further up the hillside with the occasional stell or disused lime kiln. Dorthgill farmhouse is abandoned, but the barn is kept in use for sheep and cattle fodder. Some attempts are being made to drain the boggy areas. Other farms on the Garrigill road are Hill House. Deep in the valley on the river is Hole House, where Raistrick thought the Romans obtained lead. Then come Over Lee House, Middle and Low Lee Houses, the latter having the Riding Stables. An angled bridge takes the road over the Crossgill and at the approach to Garrigill a lane goes down to the ford below the weir. Debris on the bushes show how high the waters can rise when in spate. The fine farmhouse here carries the date 1750.

29. Garrigill Church.

The church is dedicated to St John and was built about 1790 with nave and chancel in one. Later a dividing arch was put in and the windows were altered. An interesting relic is what could be a portable font, hollowed from one stone with a cross on each side. In 1935 after a further restoration of the building, a service was held to celebrate the centenary of the death of Westgarth Forster, the well known geologist and mine surveyor. He was born in 1772 locally, and his father was a mining agent and assistant manager of the Allendale and Coalcleugh mines. His son trained under him and proved so capable that on his father's death, he took over. He knew the area very well and had made surveys

58

and plans. He lived at Ivy House, Garrigill, which was also a farm. After some ten years he gave up the agency to concentrate on farming and geological survey. In 1809 appeared *A section of the Strata from Newcastle upon Tyne to Cross Fell* — in other words, along the whole course of the Tyne, a great pioneer work which was gratefully received by both geologists and miners. He went on to do professional surveying in many English counties and abroad. In 1821 appeared a second edition of his work; for many years it was a standard work. He was buried in Garrigill churchyard and was long remembered.

Garrigill is a pleasant stone village, with houses carrying dates as far back as 1621. At Lonning Head, Palmer visited the old farm house, built in bastle style. Here, however, the owners and the animals went through the same door to different apartments on the ground floor. Bewick's Cherryburn farmhouse is very like this. At Garrigill the South Tyne burbles over the stones on its way through the village, built about a green, where the inn is called the George and Dragon. There are several chapels and to the west along the Pennine Way, past a Girls' School dated 1850, is the now deserted Congregationalist Chapel at Redmire. It carries the date 1756 over the door, but it could have been an earlier building converted — a strong house or a barn. It measures 40 feet by 24 feet with a lean-to at the north end. There are four round-headed windows on the sunny side. Pevsner reported the pews and reading desk still within the buildings. It is now boarded up, surrounded by trees, and the only visiting flock is of local sheep. In a strange way it is a fascinating building, reminding us of the hard life in these parts. The graveyard monuments seem unusually large, like obelisks. one given the sad particulars of the children of William and Sarah Brown of Ivy House, Garrigill.

Phoebe and Rebecca, born and died February 6th, 1875. Josephine Pickering, born 26 January, died 29 June, 1876. Josephine Elizabeth, born 30th June, 1877, died 16 January, 1878. 'For such is the kingdom of Heaven'.

On a cold day the lambs are crying in the fields.

The chapel is very near to the spoil heaps of a lead mine, which the Pennine Way passes. Sometimes colourful pieces of fluorspar can be found — it was considered waste in former times.

The Pennine Way follows the west bank of the river for two miles and crosses a footbridge near Sillyhall Farm, then takes pleasant pathway by the river to Alston. Whether on the west or east side of the river the motorist has to face ways that wind and get narrow, rise and dip to reach Alston Townfoot or Towntop respectively. Both should be tried for the difference of view.

Alston

Alston is a convergence of routes and rivers The Middleton and Nenthead roads join on the east side of the South Tyne. The Penrith and Brampton road joins on the west side and enters the town at a lower level over the bridge. The Haydon Bridge road continues northwards, and a winding way to Nenthead branches eastwards from it. On the west side of the road is a place called Moscow and a hamlet called Ayle. There are a number of footpaths and the Alston area is excellent for walking. Information can be obtained at the old Railway Station, which is now the Tourist Information Centre. The South Tynedale narrow gauge railway runs regularly about a mile each way to the Northumberland border at Gilderdale. It crosses the Tyne Viaduct and the route can also be followed by footpath. Alston itself can be explored from this lower level. The ironworks on tbe Nent have been closed and the Nent Level adit has been blocked. The back alleys can be investigated at different levels. There are old stone houses with heavy stone slate roofs. There was once a woollen mill in Alston. Up the cobbled main street is a variety of shops and hostelries. Some fine houses of the seventeenth and eighteenth centuries can be seen: some carry dates on the doorheads.

The Town Hall was built in 1857 in Gothic style with a tower. The architect was Higham of Newcastle, and the building is an indication of the town's prosperity at that time as a market and industrial centre. A new church had been built in 1796, but this was replaced a century later (1870) by one designed by J. W. Walton. The steeple was added in 1886, giving it great prominence in the highest market town in England.

The Market Cross was erected in 1764 by Sir William Stephenson, Lord Mayor of London, who was born at Crosslands in Alston parish. Over two hundred years it had been worn, battered and rebuilt, another tribute to local pride. It is situated where the cobbled street widens and turns at an angle. The street continues to rise, but not steeply. The old Friends' Meeting House of 1732 is a reminder of the London Lead Company. The Samuel King Grammar School (1828) is no longer used as a school, but Alston has a Comprehensive High School which is said to have the smallest number of pupils in England. There is a splendid view back down the main street with the buildings falling away beneath each other and the church spire rising above all in the name of St Augustine.

Sopwith wrote that he crossed the Tyne Bridge at Alston, *near which is a shot tower (for making lead shot for guns), which with embrasures at the top and a house adjoining, has much the appearance of a church. It is 56 feet high and is built over a shaft of nearly the same depth. The shot is brought out by a level at the base of the steep hill on which the tower is built.* He went on a walk of two miles to the Ayle Burn to examine the rock strata, *scenery and singular caverns which here occur.* Here he explored a limestone cavern 20 to 30 feet high, through which the Ayle water flowed. Other caverns were discovered and in one was a great waterfall, the noise being greatly magnified. The caves were discovered in the process of leadmining, and he describes the celebrated lead mine of Hudgill Burn, drainage of water allowing access to further caverns. The flowing of water helped the ventilation and visitors were allowed, travelling so far in ore wagons, pulled by ponies. Different levels could be reached by climbing cross-sticks up or down a shaft. Another method was to sit on a bar attached to a rope, which was hauled up by a windlass. Candles were used for lighting.

Near the junction of the Ayle Burn and the Tyne is Randalholme Hall. This was originally a Border-type tower with a vaulted basement and corner stair, changing on the first floor to a different corner, from which it ascends to the top within the thickness of the wall. A substantial hall wing was added later. It has an heraldic tablet over the door with a Latin motto and initials with date G R R 1746.

Not far away is another old tower — Clargyll Hall. The stepped gables and a hall with Gothic windows were designed and built by the Revd. Octavius James, a rector of Kirkhaugh, which is situated over the Northumberland border. The church contains memorials to the local families of Ricardson and Featherstonhaugh, who lived at Randalholm and Barhaugh. Hodgson describes Kirkhaugh as having a 40 feet nave and 10 feet chancel with a medieval west window, but other windows seem eighteenth century. It had a bell cote with weather cock. There were Roman stones about and the shaft of a cross used as a gate post. Later 1868-9, called Holy Paraclete, it was rebuilt by the Revd. Octavius James, who designed the building himself without help of an architect. He kept the thirteenth century window, but added an 'absurdly thin needle spire'. (Pevsner). But Morris comments 'a spiralet of the most extraordinary needle-like slenderness'.

30. South Tyne on the Cumbrian Border.

The South Tyne in this area is particularly beautiful — the waters fringed by native trees with hills on either bank. The hills to the east provide for the Tyne

61

on this side, but over the top eastwards are the sources of East and West Allen and further still Derwent waters, that eventually join the Tyne. The line of the old railway keeps to the South Tyne on the west side of it to Lambley, but on the west side of the main road is the Roman fort of Whitley Castle, which dominated communications with the Maiden Way leading on to the Roman Wall.

Whitley Castle

A Roman fort, it was described by Sopwith as 'lozenge-shaped', the sides measuring 150 yards and 128 yards, and, *the total area including the escarpments and the ditches, amount to nine acres. On the north side are 4 and on the west side 7 ditches, in remarkably good preservation, the former extending in breadth, from the summit of the station about 40 yards and the latter 90,* The Lort Burn flowed by the north side and the Maiden Way went 50 yards to the south with the Tyne not very far away. Hodgson, who came several times, could see very little masonry of the walls, but there was a bath house outside the northern ditches, which had been partly excavated, showing the soot encrusted pillars of the hypocaust. Various inscribed Roman stones had been found.

He wrote — *Sept 5 1826, the proprietor of Whitley Castle has found a large dunghill, resembling a peat bog and which he uses for manuring his ground. It abounds with old shoes, all made right and left — those of the men clinker built — those of the ladies, without nails, but having long ears for lace holes and under each hole a fringe of leather thongs...also an abundance of fragments of earthenware.*

Two years later he excavated the midden and found more hob-bailed boots and ladies shoes. The pottery was both the Samian red ware and black ware, which was used for cooking purposes. The Samian ware was much better quality. He also found timber, grain and what he thought the bedding of horses. The discoveries were very similar to those at Vindolanda in recent years, which are so important. It is quite likely that there were fragments of writing tablets at Whitley Castle, which passed unnoticed. When transferred by the farmer to the fields as manure they would soon disappear. So quite a lot has been lost from the fort.

John Wallis, the antiquarian, was born at Castle Nook below Whitley Castle in 1733, *Being Roman ground (he said) I was led by a sort of enthusiasm to an enquiry and search after their towns, their cities and temples, their baths, their altars, their tumuli, their military ways and other remains of splendour and magnificence, which will admit of thousand views and reviews and still give pleasure to such as have a gust (taste) for anything Roman.*

The churches in the valley had collected Roman altar stones, and there were other reminders of Roman occupation. Though nowadays there is very little corn grown in these parts, in medieval times and later they had to provide for themselves — hence the name Barhaugh, from the Old English word 'bere' meaning barley. The fields in the valley were fertile, but the high ground was suitable only for summer pastures. In this area the old shielings or huts have been found, unadopted by lead miners. Hodgson wrote that because of the badness of roads and steepness of the slopes, sledges were used for transport rather than carts and pack animals were much favoured. The railway came and has gone, but the track can be followed through the valley, and the bridges are monuments of industrial archaeology. Hodgson also mentions that in October 1829 a great flood of the Tyne did great damage to the land, and in some parts forged a new bed for the river. Great boulders were moved along and deposited elsewhere; these are a great feature of the valley and beyond them the trees grow strongly.

Slaggyford

The next village Slaggyford was at one time larger than Alston. It was a market centre and noted for its annual fair on the second Saturday in July. but the lead mines took people away and the village declined. It was not an area for lead mining, and one inhabitant lost all his wealth in a vain endeavour to discover valuable minerals. Heaps of 'slag' have been found, however, accounting for the name. The village is pleasant with some fine stone houses. It is also interesting to see how road and railway and river interact — crossing over and under to suit terrain.

Knarsdale

The next settlement is Knarsdale, formerly spelt Knaresdale. It gets its name from the Knarr Burn, and Knarr means 'rugged rock'. The tradition is that a Yorkshire teacher came to the school in these parts and insisted in the insertion of the 'e' for proper spelling. It reminded him of his native county. The hostelry here was called the Kirk Style Inn and was important as the only inn for miles around, since the landowner was an ardent teetotaller and would allow no sales of liquor on his lands. The inn at Knarsdale is close to the church and is now called The Sportsman.

The church is dedicated to St Jude, and Hodgson saw it in a ruinous condition with a lot of stone lying about. It had been rebuilt in the seventeenth century, and old grave slabs were used in the building. In 1833, however, it was rebuilt at a cost of £300 and a new rectory was erected at this time. On the south wall of the church, beneath the sundial, is a stone carved with *Erected 1833. Rev. Thomas Bewsher, Rector. William Parker and Joseph Richardson, Church Wardens. Enlarged 1882. Vestry and Porch added 1906.* There is a fine collection of gravestones and one, now badly eroded, carried a strange inscription, which Hodgson called 'disgraceful doggerel'.

> *All you who please these lines to read*
> *It will cause a tender heart to bleed:*
> *I murdered was upon the fell,*
> *And by a man I knew full well;*
> *My bread and butter which he'd lade,*
> *I, being harmless, was betrayed.*
> *I hope he will rewarded be,*
> *That laid the poison here for me.*

It was the epitaph of Robert Baxter, who died October 4th, 1796. A man with whom he had a quarrel, left a poisoned wrapped sandwich for him. There is no record of the offender being brought to justice, and it is surprising that such an epitaph was allowed in the churchyard. There is another sad incident about the

63

church. Thomas Todhunter, cleric here from 1800 to 1826 was found frozen to death in a field of turnips.

31. Knaresdale Hall.

The manor of Knarsdale was held in medieval times by the Swinburn family, and in 1313 Hugh de Swinburn was rector of Knarsdale. It was later held by the Wallis family, who sold it in 1730 to John Stephenson, a Newcastle merchant. One of the Stephenson family built Alston market cross. But in 1769 Knarsdale was sold to James Wallace, a distinguished lawyer. His son Thomas, for services to his country, was created Baron Wallace of Knarsdale. The family also owned Featherstone Castle, and Hodgson described Knarsdale Hall as having declined in importance — *a gentleman's place of the C 17th now and for a long time since occupied by the farmer of the adjoining grounds...The garden walls have lost their trimness, the malt kilns and the brewhouse are gone.* Today, however, the stone buildings on top of a high mound dominate the scene and are strongly built. The mullioned windows seem to have been inserted into an older hall. A grim story is told about the place. The elderly owner lived with his nephew and niece. He married a young wife, who fell in love with the nephew and was unfaithful to her husband. This was known by the niece, and the guilty pair contrived her fall, on a dark and stormy night, into the old fish pond. They were scared by her long-haired ghost that appeared, dripping water — the nephew fled and the wife went mad. This is one of a number of ghost stories recounted on the South Tyne.

There is an interesting account of a family christening in 1838.

On June 16th, Mr J. Dickinson of Eals, in the parish of Knarsdale, Northumberland, collected together 30 of his friends and neighbours to become sponsors for his 8 children. After breakfast the party set out for church, Dickinson, who was a musician played several of his favourite airs on the violin at the head of the merry group, the mother bringing up the rear with the youngest child in her arms. They were met at the church by the Rev. Thomas Bewsher, the Rector, who christened the 8 children, observing that in all his ministry, he never before had had such a presentation.

64

and the Blenkinsopps moved to Bellister. In 1542, though still the property of John Blenkinsopp it was decayed in the roof and not in good repair.

34. Bellister Castle.

The tower had a vaulted basement about 53 feet in length and 30 feet in breadth. It also had an outer wall some four paces from the tower and surrounding it, like Middleham in Yorkshire. The wall was as high as the tower, but this by the time of the description had lost its upper storey (roofless). The outer wall to the west was removed when used for housing labourers. Then in the early nineteenth century a new house was built to the south front as the residence of the agent of the neighbouring colliery. The castle had been built from Roman Wall stone — carved and inscribed stones have been found. Once again the secret tunnel to Thirlwall Castle is a legend, since it would have to go under the river. As at Bellister, it was the drainage system to the river. Blenkinsopp was also moated. The restored Blenkinsopp Castle had and still has attractive lawns and gardens. It is supposed to have a ghost, the 'White Lady', who wanders about looking for her lost treasure chest and her lord, Brian de Blenkinsopp.

There are a number of Blenkinsopp monuments in Haltwhistle Church — one the effigy of Thomas de Blenkinsopp, and other stones carry the Blenkinsopp arms — a band between three sheaves of corn. There is a nineteenth century Blenkinsopp Hall on the north side of the Carlisle Road, and the Roman Wall is not far away. In fact it accompanies the River Tyne at a distance to Wallsend. Hadrian's Wall was designed and located with special reference to the Tyne. Only towards the mouth of the Tyne was the river a barrier, and it was a means of communication by water as far as Corbridge. The Tyne Valley was very fertile and good for corn growing, so that Roman troops could be supplied with crops that were gathered locally. Excavations have shown that at practically every Roman fort excavated, the ground beneath bore evidence of plough marks, showing that even before the Romans came, a lot of corn was grown. Again, in medieval times, there were many fields of corn in the lower areas and much in the Tyne Valley.

Haltwhistle

The name of Haltwhistle has nothing to do with a railway stop. It is literally Hal-twysel meaning 'a meeting of the streams by the hill'. Twizell is a meeting of the waters and here the Haltwhistle Burn from the north meets the Tyne, which has come down from the south and turned eastwards. The Tipalt Burn flows in from the west to add to the waters. Hodgson wrote — *Indeed the Carlisle Railway, which has its summit level in this parish at 450 feet, traverses the whole breadth of it, through highly cultivated ground.*

Haltwhistle belonged for many years in medieval times to Scottish Kings and during the wars with Scotland, it was subject to attacks. Fortified places were Castle Hill and two separate towers. One, still standing, appears as the Red Lion Hotel. Others have disappeared and Castle Hill has no outstanding stonework, but earthworks can be made out. The Haltwhistle Burn helps the defensive position. A tower is mentioned in the 1415 list, and in 1542 one is described as the property of Sir William Musgrave and kept in good repair. Hodgson mentions that there were two tower houses, then both inns, and there were others partly fortified. One carried the date 1607 and initials R W N, presumed Ridleys.

In 1598 the Scottish outlaws made an attack on the town.

They came and set many houses of the town on fire and took away all their goods; and as they were running up and down the street with lights in their hands to set more houses on fire there was one other of the Ridleys that was in a strong house, that made a shot out at them and it was his goodhap to kill an Armstrong, one of the sons of the chiefest outlaw They made off and vowed vengence, but when they came again many were captured and brought to justice.

Well constructed, stone-built houses are still a feature of central Haltwhistle, and though there are none outstanding architecturally the general appearance of the groups is good. The houses were built of local stone, but with the railway, other materials could be brought in. Haltwhistle was a market town for the exchange of local goods. In the eighteenth century two Quakers set up a baize manufactury and there was a weaving establishment. On the Haltwhistle Burn were fulling mills, dyeing and spinning mills. A walk along this stream to the Roman Wall, shows that it must have been a hive of industry with quarries, coal mining and lime burning kilns. The Directory of 1822 (Pigot) gives a whole range of craftsmen, shopkeepers and traders — 60 in number, including makers of clogs. The weekly market was held on Thursdays and there were fairs on May 14th and November 22nd for cattle and sheep.

The Church of the Holy Cross is situated below the Market Place with views over the river and the valley. It is a good example of a North Country church, impressive considering the time when it was built in the thirteenth century. The chancel measures 46 feet by 20 feet, with lancet windows — combined three lights in the east end and four single lights on each side, the walls being supported by buttresses. Inside is a piscina (for washing) and three sedilia (seats for the clergy). There are a number of medieval grave covers to Blenkinsopps and Thirlwells. A monument to John Ridley of Walltown, who died in 1562 begins,—

Ihon Redle that sum tim did be
Then lard of the Wal Ton
Gon is he out of thes val of mesre
His bons lies under this ston
We must believe be Gods mersy
Into this world gave hes son
Then for to redem al Chrestens...

The nave measures 63 feet by 46 feet and has side aisles above which are clerestory windows. It has four bays with round columns and pointed arches, looking very spacious inside. The font, dated 1676, has some curious crude carvings on it, and there is another large circular bowl on a shaft, which is probably an earlier font. At the west end it has long lancet windows and a bell-cote, again typical of the North country.

* John Ridley that some time did be then lord of the Walltown. Gone is he out of this vale of misery. His bones lie under this stone. We must believe by God's mercy. Into this world he gave His son Then to redeem all Christians.

Crossing the waters

Crossing the Tyne always presented a difficulty, and in 1776 Hutchinson wrote of this — *We proceed towards Haltwezell in hopes to pass the river by ferry boat; but the boatman, who thinks himself a competent judge of the necessity there is for his attendance, was not to be found; and we were obliged to pass the ford, which is broad and deep, with a bottom of large stones, over which the horse, breast deep in water, unaccustomed to the passage, incessantly faulters or stumbles'* They managed to get a guide, but this shows the dangers.

We ourselves have seen both the difficulties and hazards. The South Tyne and its tributaries, like the East and West Allen, in time of flood roll the boulders along. The smaller stones are moved further and more easily. The larger pile up along one bank, and it is very difficult to climb down the boulders to the water. Bridges are infrequent and fords require a flat pavement of rock. A girl had left her cardigan on one bank and had crossed the river further up by a suspension bridge. When her attention was called to her lost garment, she decided to walk over in what seemed shallow water, bare-foot. She flopped into the water several times on the wet stones, also pinching her feet. By the time she got over she was soaking wet. This was in dry weather when the water was low. In an area not far away, the river, in time of spate, had carved out one bank bringing down piles of stone and several large trees.

Thomas Bewick in his wood-cuts has a whole number of illustrations showing the crossings of the river — the ferry boats, the bridges, the fords, a man walking over on stilts and, strangely, a man trailing behind his cow holding its tail and thus avoiding the payment of toll. The animal gave him security; four feet are safer than two when crossing the river.

There are several fords over the South Tyne between Haltwhistle and Haydon

Bridge. There is a footbridge crossing at Bardon Mill Station and the only bridge for traffic is near Crow Hall, above the junction of Tyne and Allen waters, leading to Ridley Hall and Beltingham, which is a most beautiful area. There is a metalled road back along the south bank to Williemoteswick Castle, but beyond that the roads are farm tracks and it is better walking than riding.

Willimoteswick Castle

Willimoteswick presents a most impressive picture whether from the main road or the railway. The castle overlooks the South Tyne and to the south the rather empty land rises high to Ridley Common. The enclosure of the farm, formerly the barmkin, is approached by a strong gatehouse and within are grouped the house and the farm buildings. It is famous as the birthplace of Bishop Nicholas Ridley, who was burnt at the stake in 1555, during the reign of Mary Tudor. In 1542 the fortification was described as a 'good tower and stone house adjoining thereto, of the inheritance of Nicholas Ridley and kept in good reparations'.

35. Willimoteswick Castle.

The Gatehouse measures 40 feet by 22 feet with very thick walls. It has a carriage entrance ten feet wide with barholes for a stout wooden bar behind the doors. Within are two doorways to the north, one leading to the guardroom and tho other to the spiral stairway. This rises through three storeys to the roof which has a parapet, and the battlements project on corbelling. Some of the waterspouts are fashioned to look like guns. Within the walls the main room has an original fireplace, extending to a width of eleven feet. From the roof extensive views can be obtained, and in olden times this would be good for security. The original windows were very narrow, but here are later insertions. There is a recess above the entrance which probably carried the Ridley coat of arms. The original hall or manor house within the enclosure has been very much altered though the ages. The great fireplace is there and thick walls. At either end are tall towers, 40 feet high looking like chimneys. They measure 17 feet by

8 feet with a slight batter. At one time they had battlements and stairs within. One had a garderobe and both are strongly built. Extra buildings were added to the manor house. An inventory of 1585 lists the rooms as Inner Chamber, Great Chamber, Chamber over the stairhead, other chambers for servants, Parlour Buttery, Kitchen and Hall. Possessions included *20 pairs of double linen sheets, ten pairs of 'strakings' sheets, ten pairs of 'harne' sheets, six 'wishons', six 'worset wishons', six candlesticks, a new cupboard, a 'hurle' bed, a new 'presser', seven chests, two 'carping cloths', two cupboard cloths, four new sacks, a Bible and the 'Boke of Marters', written by Johne Foxe, including a vivid account of the martyrdom of Bishop Ridley.*

The Ridley's were, and still are, an important Northumberland family. Some followed the Tyne to Newcastle and prospered as merchants and landowners. Blagdon became their seat with the first Viscount Ridley emerging at the turn of the century. The present Nicholas Ridley was a minister in Mrs Thatcher's government until his recent resignation.

Beltingham

There may have been a private chapel at Willimoteswick, but the nearest church is in the attractive village of Beltingham. It is dedicated to St. Cuthbert and stands in a churchyard containing three massive yew trees, which are more than 700 years old, and may well have been used for the making of longbows before guns came. Bishop Nicholas Ridley was keen on archery, which was compulsory school sport in the days of Henry VIII. The yew tree indicates an old church, but the present church was built about 1500 in perpendicular style. There is no division between nave and chancel, and the roof carries a little bell tower. There is an old cross shaft at the west end. In 1883-4 the church was very much restored, and some of the old memorials were destroyed. One, recorded by Hodgson, requested prayers for the soul of Nicholas Ridley, who died in the fifteenth century (1490), the last part of the year being destroyed. There is a memorial now in the church to the Revd. Anthony Hedley of Chesterholm, friend of John Hodgson, who died 17th January 1835, having caught a fatal chill in going out to supervise an excavation at Vindolanda fort.

He was born near Otterburn and related to Capability Brown. Both had served the Marquis of Bath at Longleat. Hedley was inspired to improve vicarage gardens as well as to search for antiquities. He was curate at Gateshead and vicar of St. John Lee (overlooking The Tyne); He was curate in Newcastle and Whitfield. He excavated at Whitley Castle as well as Chesterholm, and went with Hodgson to the Roman Wall to excavate.

As stated, Beltingham is a most attractive village with stone houses about a little green with pretty flowering gardens. There is a fine Georgian house near the church, and another nearby looks as if it had been a bastle. On the way to Ridley Hall is yet another, which was called Ivy Cottage. Some years ago the basement was still used as a store. It has been modernised, but the original entrance is still there, built of Roman stone, with a great slab as a lintel, the hole in which shows that it was once a door step with the socket holes for the door. Local legend has it that it was used by bowmen for target practice. Perhaps their yews came from Beltingham churchyard.

73

Ridley Hall

Surrounded by parkland trees, lawns and gardens, Ridley Hall has a most attractive setting. Some of the land here is now the property of the National Trust and the kitchen garden of the Hall, which still keeps lawns and trees, is used as a car park. From here there are walks along both sides of the river Allen, which joins the Tyne below Ridley Bridge, constructed in 1792. Ridley Hall was once owned by the Ridleys, but acquired by the Lowes. In 1773 William Lowes built a fine mansion house here. Overlooking the River Allen, it was surrounded by trees, with lawns and gardens before the house. From the higher ground there were extensive views of the countryside, varying from the enclosed gardens, the tree girt valleys to the high hills. Neighbouring establishments could be seen, 'scenes at once beautiful, grand and romantic'. (Mackenzie).

The house was rebuilt in 1891 in neo-Tudor style and re-used materials were brought into the interior, including a Jacobean overmantel from Mottisfront Abbey, Hampshire. There is also some re-used panelling. For a time it belonged to the Bowes-Lyon family, who gave 185 acres of Allen Banks and the kitchen garden to the National Trust. The Hall is now used by Northumberland County as a residential education centre.

36. Ridley Bridge.

Tyne Floods

When considering the crossings of the Tyne, we are forcibly reminded of the great floods of November 1771, which swept away all the bridges except the one at Corbridge.

37. 1771 Flood — Fate of Newcastle Bridge.

A report of November 17th reads *About 2 o'clock in the morning of this day (Sunday), the inhabitants of Newcastle were alarmed with the most dreadful inundation that ever befel that part of the country.* The water was 6 feet higher than the previous highest flood, and all the buildings near the river were completely under water. The flood was so sudden that people escaped with difficulty from the lower parts. The old Tyne bridge of 9 arches had houses built along it. The middle arch gave way under pressure of the waters, and then 2 arches on the Gateshead side. Seven houses and shops with some people were carried away. Next day four more houses and shops fell into the water. The house of Mr Patten, a mercer, was carried down to Jarrow Slake, where it stuck like Noah's Ark. Inside were found two animals — a cat and a dog, seemingly no worse for the experience. A Mr Fiddes with his wife, a maid and two children were left stranded on top of a crumbling pier in perishing cold till 10 am. They were saved by a bricklayer, who broke through shops still standing and got planks across the gap. The water had risen more than 12 feet above the high water mark for spring tides. The Sandhill was under 6 feet of water — timber and the produce of merchants were swept away. A lot of keels, boats and small craft were snatched by the flood waters and carried away to be wrecked on the rocks of Tynemouth or Shields, or swept out to sea. Three sloops and a brig were deposited on the Quay, doing much damage. The water had poured down from all sources in great torrents, all the tributaries combining into a great Tyne flood. *Newcastle did not alone suffer by the terrible violence of this flood, scarcely a village or cottage house from Tynehead in Alston Moor to Shields escaped its destructive fury. The bridges at Alston, Ridley Hall, Haydon, Chollerford and Hexham were all carried away by the torrent and many people were drowned: a prodigious quantity of horses, black cattle, sheep & other animals perished. The wooden bridge, at Allen-*

dale, was swept away entire and was discovered next day lying across a lane near Newbrough, as exactly as if fixed there by human means.

At Haydon Bridge the whole town was under water, and men waded up to the neck carrying chidren to the sanctuary of the church. At West Boat, where the ferry was, near Hexham, a man saved himself and his family by making a hole in the thatch of the roof of his house and climbing out. At Warden the water level had risen 13 feet. In the valley corn stacks were washed away the great damage done. *The beautiful bridge at Hexham, consisting of 7 arches and which had only been finished the year before, with great rejoicings, was totally demolished during the night.*

The bridge at Corbridge, built in 1674, survived; and it was thought to be built on Roman foundations. The Roman bridge, however, was near Corstopitum and had gone long ago. The level of the water here can be imagined today, since at that time some daring onlookers were able to lean over the wall and dip their hands in the flood. It was the width of the bridge that saved it. It has seven arches and the river here is very wide.

Beyond Corbridge, Bywell was the next place to suffer terribly. Here the whole of the village was under deep water, and in Mr Fenwick's mansion house, it was eight feet deep. His most important possessions were his race-horses. Bywell had a famous stud, and the horses were saved by taking them to refuge in St. Peter's Church, the highest point of the village. An unusual stable, it kept the horses safe while the cattle, sheep, corn and hay were swept along by the flood. It seems that the horses stood upon the pews and the tops were gnawed by them. One enterprising horse saved itself by getting upon the altar. Bywell had more houses in those days, but they were swept away. Many people were saved by being rescued from roofs, and others held on to the trees, but six people were drowned. St. Andrew's Church suffered badly — the churchyard wall was swept away and much of the churchyard. "Dead bodies and coffins were torn out of the churchyard and the living and the dead promiscuously clashed in the torrent". Church fittings and records were lost and immense damage done. Bywell bridge also went down and the weir was shattered.

At Ovingham there were ten people in the boat-house that night — there was a ferry but no bridge. When the waters came into the house, they went upstairs and broke a way into the stable which was more strongly built. The house was swept away and in time the stable went. The people were swept away with the roof timbers and the thatch. Three of them managed to get into trees and were saved after ten hours, but the rest perished. Wylam colliery was completely flooded, and devastation caused all down the river to the sea. Ships were wrecked, but the strangest survival was a baby, floating in a wooden cradle.

At Newcastle the bridge continued to crumble and six more shops and houses fell into the river. All the houses from the south bank to the blue stone (the Durham boundary) on both sides of the bridge had been demolished and it was necessary to build a new bridge. It is difficult to estimate the chaos and the damage caused by these floods. County Durham was similarly affected. This was the worst flood, but there were others as March 10th, 1782.

There was a great fall of snow and next morning a very heavy rain, with a strong

Chapter Four
HEXHAM

43. View of Hexham.

Hexham is central to the County of Northumberland, being about half way between Tynemouth and Carlisle. In the mid eighteenth century communications were enormously improved by the construction of the Military Road along the east west route and the Alemouth or Corn Road to the coast at Alnmouth, then a flourishing port and with plenty of corn to be exported.

Hexham has had a turbulent history, being destroyed by the Danes and the Scots on several occasions. It was also subject to raids of the Border Reivers and their history is displayed in the Middle March Centre, at one time the prison of the Archbishop of York. Hexhamshire was a 'regality' of the Archbishop in the same way that Durham, Bedlingtonshire, Norham and Islandshire were to the Bishop of Durham. Saint Wilfrid, built the first church in Hexham about 673, which was then considered to be the finest north of the Alps. It was built of Roman stone and can be seen by entering the crypt of Hexham Abbey. The limits of this church have been traced by excavation. It was a monastic church and was rebuilt between 1180 — 1250. Much of this structure is still there, but most of the monastic buildings were destroyed after the Dissolution of the Monastery in 1536, which caused a riot in the town. The area of the cloister can be seen south of the nave, and in the neighbouring park are the remains of a medieval bridge over the Cockshaw Burn, which flows under the gardens by a tunnel. The stream probably provided water for the Abbey — monastic institutions had the same care for sanitation as the Romans in their forts.

85

44. Abbey Gate at Hexham.

The Abbey Church was restored in the last century in the same style, but the old stonework is evident and much more attractive. Within the Abbey can be seen the Midnight Stairs down which the monks used to descend from their dormitory for the night time services. At the bottom of the stairs is a monument to Flavinus, standard bearer to a Roman cavalry regiment. He is depicted riding down a barbarian, but it seems that he fell in battle — hence the memorial. There is also part of a shaft of a carved Anglo Saxon cross, attributed to Bishop Acca. Another fine possession is the Saxon frith stool or Bishop's chair. The interior of the church is very spacious, and viewed from the Midnight Stairs is most impressive with light coming through the long lancet windows. The crypt below the floor once contained holy relics that attracted pilgrims, who could come and pray for help and health. The painted roodscreen, dividing nave and chancel, was erected in the fifteenth century. The chancel stalls have misericordes with carved tipping seats. There are two Chantries with delicate screens and painted panels. The Leschman Chantry has some lively and powerful carvings and there are a number of interesting monuments. There is much to see in this church and outside; on Giles Gate is the gatehouse of the monastery. This presumes a walled precinct for the abbey and the area to the south east of the church is the marketplace.

The Shambles or Market shelters were built in 1776 by Sir Walter Blackett, who held the Lordship of the Manor, which he purchased from the Fenwicks and later transferred to the Beaumonts by marriage. Colonel Beaumont had a house at the west end of the church.

The east side of the market is dominated by the Moot Hall, which was a medieval tower of the Archbishop of York, and a second tower beyond it was the prison. Still beyond this are buildings dated 1674, which was the Queen Elizabeth I Grammar School, founded in 1599. There was a school formerly connected with the monastery, which was destroyed by the Scots.

86

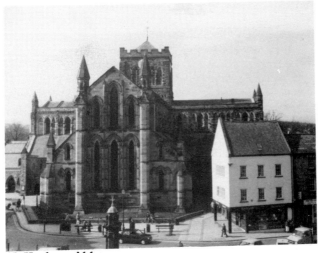

45. Hexham Abbey.

46. Hexham Market Place.

This hilltop town is most impressive in its situation, and has been likened to an Etruscan hill town. Some fine old stone houses line the main street. Celia Fiennes, visiting in 1698, wrote — *This is one of the best towns in Northumberland except Newcastle..... its built of stone & looks very well, there are two gates to it, many streets some are pretty broad all well pitch'd with a spacious market place with a town Hall on the Market Crosse......* From the hilltop there are extensive views across the river and the countryside — meadows, trees and the more distant hills.

The roads make a steep descent down Gilligate to the industrial quarter, where the Cockshaw Burn still flows down the street. Wright (1823) wrote — *The suburb of Cockshaw is divided into several narrow streets. The brook flows through its centre and is crossed and recrossed by little bridges. The houses are generally mean and there is nothing interesting or curious. Here the tanneries and most of the glove manufactories are situated.*

Hexham had been long famous for its manufacture of leather. Wright gives some statistics — *77 men & boys employed as Leather dressers and Glove-cutters, 40 boys employed as Dusters and 1,111 women employed as Sewers.*

Skins dressed annually were 80,000, and 18,000 skins of dressed leather were imported. From these were made and exported annually 23,504 dozens of pairs of gloves. Dutch Oker was used in the processing, but local fell clay could be used if necessary.

Tanning was a necessary allied industry and there were four tanneries, employing a score of men. In a year they dealt with 5,000 hides and 12,000 calf skins. They supplied local saddlers, bootmakers and cobblers.

Hexham also had 16 master hatters, and the trade employed 40 persons. There were two woollen manufactories, worked by steam power and two rope manufactories. There were corn water mills below the bridge. A windmill on the Seal was ruinous, but there was one still working on Tyne Green.

47. Bridge over the Tyne at Hexham.

It was, and still is a flourishing market, including a mart for cattle and other farm animals. A canal was proposed at the beginning of the last century, but this was never realized, and the railway came on the lower level. In 1948 Honeyman was able to write that from *the meeting of the two Tynes at Hexham, the Carlisle Newcastle Railway affords a series of pictures of great beauty as it crosses and recrosses the Tyne. At every bridge a fresh stretch of river, overhung by trees, comes into view. In the spring or autumn it is almost worth while to travel to Carlisle and back to Newcastle for the scenery alone.*

There are some attractive walks along the river at Hexham — the parkland near the bridge and beyond, where the old bridges and ferry were. The old Alemouth Road can be followed on foot, passing the Hermitage, a fine eighteenth century

88

house. This is a reminder of St. John of Beverley, a local hermit and supposedly worker of miracles. The pleasing church of St John Lee on the hillside amid the trees is dedicated to him. There was a medieval church, but it was rebuilt in 1818 by Dobson and in 1885 enlarged by Hicks, so that it has a tower with spire — a landmark that can be seen from Warden, Hexham and all around. From the churchyard are magnificent views of Hexham, the Tyne and the road systems of the area.

In 1765 at St John Lee Church a most remarkable marriage was celebrated. The bridegroom was Robert Scott, a well-known Northumbrian piper. He was 90 years old and for 26 years he had moved about on crutches. His bride, Jean Middlemas, was only 25 years old and might be regarded as destined to be a nurse to a antique husband. But on his wedding day, he threw his crutches away and walked from the village of Wall, where he lived, to the church. He walked back again among a group of fellow pipers. At the conclusion of the marriage, they were all regaled with cakes and ale. Was this a miracle by St John of Beverley?

In this area there was much mining and quarrying. The coal mine at Acomb in 1886 employed 200 workers and 51,000 tons of coal per annum were raised. It was good coking coal and 41 coke ovens were in use. At Fallowfield then still working was another lead mine, where the Romans had mined and quarried. In 1886 the mine employed 120 men, mining lead and barytes. Spoil heaps and the engine house can still be seen.

Beaufront Castle

Nearby there are a number of fine country houses, the most impressive being Beaufront Castle. The property belonged to the Carnabys and then to the Erringtons. We are told that in 1715 the Earl of Derwent-water came here to persuade the owner to join the rebellion. Mr Errington pointed out to him the fine property he held across the river at Dilston and enquired whether he proposed to risk such an inheritance in a doubtful cause. The Ratcliffes of Dilston failed, but the Erringtons were able to stay on until Beaufront was purchased by W. Cuthbert. He commissioned John Dobson to build a new house and the architect obliged in the grand style (1837—41). Dobson was proud of it and considered it to be his best work. In Gothic style it is a feature of the landscape, looking like a picture with trees providing shelter belts and with gardens and meadows reaching down to the Tyne. Part of the previous Georgian house was incorporated, and some curious figures from the old buildings were placed on the north wall.

Dilston and Devil's Water

Directly opposite over the river, the site of Dilston Hall can be seen, and we follow Celia Fiennes. *Thence I went through Lord Derwentwaters parke just by his house which is an old building not very large: soe to a little village (Corbridge) where I crossed the Tyne on a long bridge of stone with many arches: at this time of the yeare being midsummer the springs are the lowest & the rivers shallow & where there is any rocks or stones quite bare of water.*

A stream called Devil's water joins the Tyne near Corbridge, and this we explore next. The name is perhaps rather misleading, since it is a most attractive little river with no Satanic associations. It flows down some 14 miles from the Allendale hills through deep ravines with tortuous turns. Since it tumbles over rocks it is often heard before it is seen. Before reaching the Tyne it passes through Dilston Haughs, meadows that are crossed by the old Roman road called Dere Street. Devil's Water passes under the Hexham Road bridge and from this point a lane leads along the river to Dilston Mill, which is still standing, an impressive piece of architecture. The water which turned the wheels now passes noisily over the rocks, and the lane continues as a private road to Dilston Hall. The area is embowered with trees and the single arched bridge over the water is most attractive and a suitable scene for the painter. It is considered one of the most delightful spots in the county.

48. Devil's Water near Dilston.

The original name of the place and the family living there was Dyvilston, abbreviated to Dilston. It was a considerable village with a manor house. No tower is mentioned in 1415, but William Claxton, who acquired the property, probably started building the fortified building that still exists. It was mentioned in 1464, and originally it measured about 40 feet by 24 feet. The basement consisted of two vaulted chambers — the larger 21½ feet by 12 feet had two loops on the east and west (longer) sides. The smaller chamber at the entrance led to the spiral stair and the two main floors above. Shortly afterwards an addition was made to the south end measuring 14½ feet by 13 feet with a door into the main building and lit by three loops. Above were small rooms with fireplaces. Then in the second half of the sixteenth century, after the Ratcliffes acquired the property, a new entrance was extended on the eastern side and another block added to the north end of the tower, which rose to four storeys, each apartment having double windows.

There was another range of buildings added on the north on plans of 1621 called the 'old hall'. A whole range was added to the east side of this and at right angles to the original tower. It consisted of six separate apartments with a central passage leading to porches on the north and south. The ground floor was mainly cellars, kitchen, pantry and stores: above were the other apartments on two storeys. The chapel to the south had also been built in this period, and the enclosed courtyard was entered by an arched gateway with the initials F R 1616 J R for Francis and Jane Radcliffe.

The village lay to the east of the castle, and beside the corn mill there was a fulling mill. The Radcliffes had a deer park at Dilston and they had other properties in Northumberland and Cumbria. During the Civil War they suffered losses, but benefitted in the reign of Charles II. Sir Edward's son, Francis married Lady Margaret Tudor, a natural daughter of the King, so they were now linked to royalty. Their son James, later the Earl of Derwentwater and his brother were sent abroad as Catholics to receive their education. They went to St. Germain's, where the expelled James II and his son were in exile. So James Radcliffe was educated along with the Pretender. In 1709, at the age of 20, the young lord returned to Dilston and made a great impression. Immediately he began rebuilding Dilston Hall on the grand scale. Invevitably in 1715 when the Pretender returned to claim the throne from George of Hanover, the young Earl of Derwentwater joined the rebels. After their defeat, he could not escape the death penalty and forefeited his life on Tower Hill, February 24 1716. There was said to be an unusually magnificent display of the Aurora Borealis over Devil's Water on the night of the Earl's death, and it has since been known as 'Lord Derwentwater's Light'.

There was immense sympathy for him, and his body was brought back to Dilston chapel for burial in the family vault. The estates for some years suffered neglect, and the property was plundered by local people. Furniture and fittings were taken away and stone used for building houses in Corbridge, including the Golden Lion public house. After being in the hands of a speculator, the lands were conferred on Greenwich Hospital, and the Hall was demolished in 1768. Only the original tower and seventeenth century house remain. John Grey of Dilston was responsible for the administration of the estates (1833—63) and built the residence that still stands.

It is at present used by Mencap, and it is hoped to raise sufficient money to restore the old buildings as a historical monument. These stand on what was the west side of the eighteenth century mansion. Mounds to the north overlooking Corbridge and eastwards where the old village was, indicate the remains of the buildings after demolition. Souvenirs and even Derwentwater's lead coffin had been stolen from the chapel.

A strange incident at Dilston was the appearance of a woman, claiming to be Amelia, Countess of Derwentwater and descended from John, son of the 3rd Earl. She occupied the ruined hall in 1868 and had to be evicted. Then she camped at the gates, providing a spectacle for curious visitors, and winning some sympathy.

A winding road from Dilston joins another similar road from Hexham above Linnold's Bridge. This once carried an inscription to the effect — *God Preserve Winfoird Erengton Belldete This Brege of Lyme And Stone An Do 1581*

91

It has a fine rainbow arch of 45 feet and a width of 10 feet between the parapets. A narrow road with two right angled bends is difficult for modern traffic. In 1684 it was out of repair and had to be partly rebuilt. Above the bridge and the junction of Devil's Water and the Dipton Burn is the site of the Battle of Hexham Levels 1464. This was where during the Wars of the Roses, Lord Montagu, in charge of the Yorkist troops, inflicted a heavy defeat on the Lancastrian troops of Henry VI. The King escaped to Bywell and the Border, but a number of Lancastrian lords were put to death. There seems to be very little historical evidence for the story of Queen Margaret facing robbers and hiding in a cave on the Dipton Burn after a previous battle.

49. Ruins of the Dukesfield lead smelter.

We might move on after exploring these waters, but it should be mentioned that at Dukesfield on the Devil's Water are the remains of a lead smelter. There are two arches of stone, lined with brick in the woods of Bywell Estates. The owners of Bywell were the Beaumonts, taking the title of Lord Allendale.

If the source of the Devil's Water at Hope Fell is traced on foot we would be near the Beldon Burn, which in turn becomes the River Derwent and marks the boundary of Northumberland and Durham.

Blanchland

Blanchland is so special that it has to be visited. It is regarded as a model village, its plan being determined by the buildings of the Premonstratensian Abbey, the abode of the White Canons, dating from 1175.

Edward III was at Blanchland in 1327 in pursuit of a Scottish army and he stayed at the Abbey. He failed to catch the enemy on account of flooded rivers which could not be crossed. The Abbey had the advowson of the Church of St Andrew at Bywell, called the 'White' church. After the Dissolution (1539), the Abbey was purchased by William Farewell, whose daughter married Cuthbert

Radcliffe. It was later acquired by the Forsters and was purchased in 1704 by Lord Crewe, Bishop of Durham, who married Dorothy Forster. The Crewe Trustees repaired the church and restored the village on the monastic site.

The remains of the monastic church, used as the village church, consist of the choir with the north transept and tower. The nave was demolished and the graveyard occupies this area. On the south side of the church was the cloister with the usual range of monastic buildings. Of these, the west range is now the Lord Crewe Arms. Adjoining the churchyard is the Abbot's tower with its vaulted basement. Next come the lodgings for visitors and the kitchen with a large fireplace. Away from this eastwards was the dining room and on the eastern side another range of buildings completed the cloister enclosure, which is now the hotel garden. To the west of the Abbot's tower stands the Gatehouse which controlled the entrance in the past to the monastic buildings, and today the Market Square. The Lord Crewe arms has a number of curious features to be explored, and you can drink in what may have been the abbot's cellar.

Within the churchyard is a cross and inside the church are several medieval grave slabs — two of abbots and two of foresters with bugles, swords, bows and arrrows. Nowadays sportsmen come from August 12th onwards to shoot grouse on the heather covered hills. In 1823 there were five lead mines near Blanchland on both sides of the Derwent, and a two-arched bridge links the counties of Durham and Northumberland. The Derwent frets over its stony bed towards Derwent Water, a modern reservoir and leisure centre. The Derwent continues for many miles as a county boundary and joins the Tyne near Blaydon. So water from the hills descends by yet another route.

Corbridge and Corstopitum

We return by road to the Tyne at Corbridge, which could be called two towns — one Roman at Corstopitum and one modern at the bridge. The name is derived from the Cor Burn which enters the Tyne opposite to the Devil's Water. The Romans must have found this a suitable place at the river crossing with the fells to the north. The Stanegate was the earlier frontier before the Roman Wall was built, and Agricola established a large military compound west of the present site.

It was excavated in part in advance of road work on the Corbridge bypass. Later a fort was established on the present site and this remained when forts were moved to the Wall. Corstopitum became a large civilian centre as well as a military base. The present part exposed to view of visitors at the English Heritage Centre is only a fragment of the town as shown on aerial photographs. There is a grid pattern of streets and houses. The Roman bridge was below the site, and barges came up the river to this important supply base. The Roman road called Dere Street ran from York through Corbridge and by Melrose to the Firth of Forth. The award winning Museum at Corstopitum with maps and plans explains the situation. Finds from periodic excavations on the site illustrate how the people of those times lived, fed and fought. There are foundations of barracks, houses, granaries, temples and a large civic centre that was never finished. It can also be seen how the town was supplied with water by aqueduct leading from the hills to a large tank which carried a sculpture of a lion killing a stag. Water could be obtained for men and horses and it continued through channels to other parts of the settlement and fort and finally to the baths, which have so far not been unearthed. The baths at Red House were used by soldiers from the large compound, erected in the process of conquest of North Britain and Caledonia, but later dismantled. From Corstopitum a view can be obtained of the Tyne and our modern communications of roads and railway. Modern Corbridge stands on high ground to the east, and most of the stone missing from the Roman town can be found in the buildings in this town.

The Anglo Saxon settlement here was also the place of a royal residence, and land was granted for the building of a monastic church dedicated to St. Andrew. It was not so large as Hexham, but built out of Roman stone. The west tower shows that there was formerly a porch, later built up into a tower. All the stone is Roman and inside the tower arch shows what kind of structures could have been seen at Corstopitum. There we only see the broken pieces, the shattered columns and arches, but here there are complete structures. Corbridge may have been the capital of Northumbria for a time and here King Aldred fought Regnald the Dane (918).

It was a place of great importance in medieval times. The church was much extended and the town grew so that it was second only to Newcastle in importance in the county. Tax assessments show that Newcastle had 297 taxpayers, Corbridge 77, Alnwick and Newbiggin next with 49. Multiplication by 20 gives the approximate population. Corbridge benefitted greatly from its situation on Dere Street, though there were disadvantages during the Scottish Wars. It was burnt in 1296 and suffered from further raids. As a borough it had its own seal and market. There was a Fair from 1293 and this continued as the famous Stagshaw Bank Fair, one of the great fairs of the country. The burgesses in 1235 built a bridge on the site of the present one. The bridge was often in need of repair and in 1674 a seven arched bridge was completed. It was severely damaged by floods in 1689, 1701 and 1713, but survived the great flood in 1771.

50. Corbridge Bridge — the only survival in 1771.

94

castle, an earthwork, can still be seen overlooking the Tyne. Styford Village suffered from Scottish attacks in olden times and here was a ford. By the eighteenth century there were only a few houses, and the Hall was rebuilt in classical style. The remaining tenants were moved across the river to Broomhaugh. The landowners of the eighteenth century liked to have areas cleared of people both for appearances and the preservation of game. When Styford was leased the lessee had *to restrain the tenants of the estate as far as they have the power from keeping hounds, greyhounds, lurchers or other dogs used for the pursuit of game.*

Riding Mill

In the nineteenth century, with the development of the railway on the south side of the river, what might be called dormitories for Newcastle business men were built.

Riding Mill had a number of shipbuilders, ship owners, lawyers and industrialists living there in substantial houses. The railway provided easy and speedy travel to work as well as quick conveyance for commodities. Mackenzie (1825) wrote — *The Riding Mill is built upon a mountain brook called Dipton Burn which it was often hazardous to pass, but in 1822 a good bridge was built across it. It is 80 feet in length and 28 feet in breadth.* In recent times the road from the south coming into Riding Mill was a notorious traffic hazard because of the steep slope and the bends. A safety pit of small stones was constructed to halt vehicles that got out of control. The hill was also difficult to climb the other way, but a new road by-passes Riding Mill.

Another recent development is a powerful pumping station that can transfer Kielder water to tunnels connecting the Tyne to the River Wear and the River Tees.

The corn mill existed in medieval times and was granted to the monastery at Blanchland. It was a good source of profit because all the tenants had to bring their corn to be ground here and hand mills were forbidden by law. Since crossing the burn was difficult a pack horse bridge was constructed 1599—1600. In recent times the mill has been converted into a residence, but its appearance has been kept. The 18 foot water wheel was of the overshot type and a dam 500 yards above the mill retained the water for its use. The large house opposite became the Wellington Hotel. It is a handsome structure and carries the date 1660 above the door. The letters are considered to be the initials of Thomas Errington and his wife Ann Carnaby. T.B. has come about by the Boultflour family living here; they were millers and probably altered the E into a B.

The house gained some notoriety by its association with witchcraft. Anne Armstrong, the witch finder, lived at Birchesnook. In 1673 she accused Anne, wife of Thomas Baites of Morpeth, a tanner, of frequenting witches' meetings at Riding Bridge-end, where she danced with the devil. She also claimed to have seen Anne Forster of Stocksfield, Anne Dryden of Prudhoe and Lucy Thompson of Mickley, supping with *'theire proctector which they called their god'* in the Riding house. But the charges were dismissed at the Morpeth Quarter Sessions, the magistrates not being impressed with the evidence.

99

The Pride of the Tyne

We now move along the Tyne into an area which became industrialised in the eighteenth century. There were a number of coal mines, iron works, kilns and waggonways, which became railways. Some of the most important men in the history of Northumberland lived hereabouts — Thomas Bewick, William Hedley, George Stephenson and Sir Charles Parsons. From them we get the steam locomotive, the turbine and the most illuminating pictorial record of life in the county during a period of great change.

Thomas Bewick was born in August 1753 at Cherryburn, a small farm on the south bank of the river Tyne, about twelve miles from Newcastle, a distance that was not unusual for walking. In his memoir Bewick describes his home *Cherryburn House, the place of my nativity, and which for many years my eyes beheld with cherished delight, is situated on the south side of the Tyne, in the County of Northumberland, a short distance from the river. The house, stables etc. stand on the west side of a little dean, at the foot of which runs a burn. The dean was embellished with a number of cherry and plum trees, which were terminated by a garden on the north. Near the house were two large ash trees growing from one root, and, at a little distance, stood another of the same kind. At the south end of the premises was a spring well, overhung by a large hawthorn bush, behind which was a holly hedge and further away was a little boggy dean with underwood and trees of different kinds. To the westward, adjoining the house, lay the common or fell which extended some few miles in length and was of various breadths.*

His father was tenant of the farm and a nearby colliery form which the family mined coal for local sale. Thomas was the eldest of eight children, and as a boy assisted the family in this work. He wrote — *From the little window at my bed head I noticed all the varying seasons of the year and when the Spring put in, I felt charmed by the music of Birds..... The chief business imposed upon me as a task at this season, was in my being set to work to scale the pastures and the meadows, that is spreading the Molehills over the surface of the ground - this and gardening and such like jobs was very hungry work.* He tells of his enjoyment of a meal, sitting under a hedge, watching the trees, the bushes and the birds. Spring *was the signal for the Angler to prepare his fishing Tackle and in doing this, I was not behind hand, with any of them in making my own all ready - Fishing Rods - Set Gads and night lines were all soon made fit for use and with them late and early I had a busy time of it during the long summer months and until the frosts of Autumn forbid me to proceed. - The uneasiness, which my late evening wadings by the water side, gave to my father and mother I have often since reflected upon with regret - they could not go to bed with the hopes of getting to sleep, while haunted with the apprehension of me being drowned and well do I remember to this day, my father's well known whistle which called me home - he went a little distance from the house, where nothing obstructed the sound and whistled so loud through his finger and thumb, that in the still hours of the evening, it might be heard echoing up the Vale of the Tyne to a very great distance......''* The whistles of locomotives were still to come.

Bewick observed the countryside carefully and later his observations were naturally recorded in his paintings and engravings — birds, beasts, flowers, trees,

The Umfravilles also held Redesdale which was claimed by the King of the Scots. In 1173 and 1174 William the Lion invaded Northumberland. He twice besieged Prudhoe Castle, but failed to take it, and the Scots vented their anger on the apple-trees. Later William the Lion was captured at Alnwick and held to ransom. Odinel de Umfraville had to rebuild and strengthen the Castle after the siege. It suffered in the Scottish Wars. In 1381 Gilbert Umfraville's widow married the Earl of Northumberland, Hotspur's father. When she died, in 1398, the Percies acquired the property. Prudhoe was forfeited at times, but recovered by the Percies. Between 1808 and 1818 the Second Duke of Northumberland restored the outer walls and the keep, but the interior was altered and a new Georgian residence was built. In recent times it has come into the care of English Heritage and is open to the public.

The Castle stands on high ground 150 feet above the Tyne and is defended by a deep dene to the east. Burns have been dammed to form a mill pond, and there is a medieval bridge on the approach to the castle. From the mill pond is a deep outer moat and the inner moat runs along the south curtain wall of the castle. Between the moats was the base court or pele-yard. Some people get confused with the word *pele*, which means enclosure and think there should be a tower here, but this area could be covered from the castle. The original castle was of earth and timber, but there were stone walls and gatehouse by the time the Scots attacked, and the keep was probably built after the attack. It is of the same style and time as that at Newcastle and very strongly built.

The approach to the castle is over the millstream bridge and the foundations of the mill are on the right. The mill pond and the pele yard are to the left, now converted to gardens. The barbican which covers the entrance is 36 feet long and 24 feet wide with a passage 11 feet wide with several doors and check points. There is a steep ascent to the gatehouse — very different from Alnwick which is on the level. The barbican ended with a drawbridge across the inner moat and worked from the fore-building of the gatehouse. The gatehouse measures 30 feet by 18½ feet and the walls on either side of the entrance passage are of solid stone-work with no chambers. The upper chamber was reconstructed as a chapel, an oriel window on the east side forming the chancel. There were lancet windows on each side. Above the chapel were two floors and the battlements with cross loops except on the north. The entrance leads to the courtyard where there would be a number of domestic buildings. Stockdale (1586) said that there was a hall 54 feet by 27 feet and another building 72 feet by 20 feet divided into two chambers with a passage between to the great tower. There was a parlour at the south end and a buttery at the north end. There was an Outer Chamber with a passage to the tower and an Inner Chamber with a passage to the chapel. Another building was called the nursery. Most of these were altered by the later building in the early nineteenth century.

The Great Tower of Keep was roughly square 41 feet from north to south, and 44 feet from east to west, but this was extended 12 feet by the fore building. The walls of the Keep are 9 feet thick and rise 45 feet to the parapet. With battlements and corner towers it would be much higher, but only one corner tower remains and the walls are much mutilated. The entrance to the tower was through the fore building, and on the ground floor are two vaulted chambers, connected with the later house for cellars, and the stairs have been altered. There were two floors above and then the battlements, with corner turrets.

The entire Castle was surrounded by a strongly built curtain wall, about 20 feet high. At the north west corner a round tower still stands to its full height. The south west corner tower has been demolished. There were turrets along the walls and a watch tower at the east end, rectangular in shape.

English Heritage has established a display centre in the Georgian house and there is much to explore. From the walls extensive views can be obtained, but we can only imagine what could be seen from the top of the keep. In many ways Prudhoe has a most interesting castle in a county famed for its fortifications. The Roman Wall is only three miles away and on the north bank of the river, crossed by a narrow bridge, is the village of Ovingham.

Ovingham Fishery

Ovingham was part of the barony of Prudhoe, and the Tyne played an important part in its history with floods that affected both the water mills and fishery. A mill and fishery are mentioned as early as 1245. A fishery like a deer park or a rabbit warren was a special privilege — a kind of game preserve granted by the King. In 1344 Gilbert Umfraville was granted a commission by Edward III to search the Tyne and destroy weirs and Kiddells (river barriers with nets for catching fish) illegally set up. The Percies at Prudhoe kept careful records of the fishery. In 1491/2 it was leased for £20 per annum, but the lessee had to keep the pool in repair and maintain the dam. Sir William Ogle, Constable of Prudhoe Castle, was given the task of searching the waters of Tyne from the pool at Ovingham to the sea. He had to take, burn and punish nets of unreasonable size. We may be surprised to hear of such regulations at this time, and it seems that the mesh of the nets was tested, so that only fish of a certain size were taken.

The detailed accounts of the bailiff show that 1503-4 — 92 salmon were sold in winter at 1s. 4d. each, but in summer, 155 were sold at 6d. each to diverse persons in the country. Trout sold at 1s. per dozen — a word used for dozen was 'seame'. The cost of upkeep of the fishery included a boat or boats, which could be used as a ferry and two fisherman who were paid £2 each. £3. 8s. 4d. was paid for 50 cartings of timber and stone for the dam by the lord's tenants and to men working on the dam. It seems that the Prior of Tynemouth had a fishery at Wylam and he was paid £2.13s4d. for the use of it in 1506/7.

Also interesting is Repairing of the fishery dam. For repairing & mending the dam of the fishery £1.13s.4d. For nets, rope & mending the boat of the fishery £2.8s. For the expenses of John Swynborne & for his trouble in overseeing the water of Tyne £1.

Paid to the clerk of the Earl's household at Leckonfield 6 barrel at 1s. 2d. a barrel, 5 bowls of white cakes, 220 salmon of the second season at 6s. the seame (12) & for the carting the same from Ovington to Newburn £6.6s.

In 1517/18 the dam was broken and had to be repaired. Thomas Donatson vicar of Ovingham was granted £12.6s.8d. *for repair of the pool. It seems that he was overseer, and from his house he was in a good position to see what was being done.*

Repairs were constantly needed, and in 1525/6, 56 wagons of stone were won from the river for this purpose. For 38 barrells bought for packing salt salmon with the packing & carriage of the same barrells £4.13s.2d.

White salt, black salt, pack thread and liquid tallow were also purchased for the fishery. The water mill was powered by water leaving the pool.

From it seems 1530 Sir Reginald Carnaby had the lease of the fishery for £3.6s.8d. and the mill for £2 yearly. He exploited the situation, cutting down far more trees than needed for the repair of the dam and more than the value of his rent.

In 1586 Stockdale mentions the fishery and the authority of the lord of Prudhoe to search all the fishers' nets from the dam of Ovingham to the sea on both sides of the river. They were to be measured and viewed and if found unlawful, burnt.

As late as 1592 the Earl was getting only £5.6s.8d. for the 'farm' or rent of the fishery and corn mill. It was worth considerably more and involved much litigation, the Earl being held prisoner in the Tower from 1605. In 1620 the fishery was leased for £60 to Thomas Thornehill, fishmonger of London, the Earl retaining the power to erect on the dam a mill or mills for the grinding of corn or for the forging and smelting of iron. In 1752 the fishery was leased at £25 a year for 25 years as fish continued to be important.

Ovingham

Ovingham village was described by Mackenzie (1825) —

It is most delightfully seated on the summit of a steep, at the foot of which glides the river Tyne. The village is tolerably well built & contains 3 farmholds, 2 inns & a brewery.....besides a number of cottages inhabited by mechanics & labourers, being the tenants of his grace the Duke of Northumberland, & each having a portion of land, which is chiefly used for growing vegetables.

The vicarage was, in medieval times, a cell for three Augustinian canons of Hexham, and was rebuilt in the seventeenth century. It is now the residence of Frank Atkinson, who did so much to establish the Beamish Museum and also the Bewick Trust at Cherryburn. Bewick received his education in the vicarage and the church. This building is yet another fine example of a church with a tall slender Anglo Saxon tower. There are fragments of a Saxon Cross in the church, which was much enlarged in the thirteenth century — wider, loftier and with long lancet windows. The nave with aisles is two bays only in length since the north and south transepts each with west aisles take up the space of two more bays. There is a long aisleless chancel with very little ornament. The churchyard has an interesting collection of gravestones in memory of village worthies.

Ovingham had a charter for a market and two annual fairs on October 26th and April 26th. There was also a monthly tryst for cattle and sheep, which was discontinued in 1823. The ceremony for the Fair was similar to Stagshaw. A procession moved to the principal alehouse for the 'riding of the fair', led by the Duke of Northumberland's pipers, dressed in light blue and adorned with the Duke's sign of a crescent moon. The procession included the Duke's agent, bailiff, constable with many farmers and tenants. The fair was proclaimed and then they beat the bounds, returning to the tavern to drink the Duke's health from punch provided by him. After this men, women and children alike went to enjoy the amusements — stalls, Punch and Judy and performers such as fire-breathers. The custom was discontinued in time, but it has been revived in recent years as the 'Goose Fair', since in the days of the old Fair geese would play an important part in the sale. Quill pens were made in Ovingham from goose feathers.

The Ovingham 'pack-horse' bridge over the Whittle Burn consists of two segmental arches with a width of five feet between the parapets, so that it could not be used for wheeled traffic. It is likely that the Ovingham mill dam on the Tyne raised the level of the water. There was a great fire at Ovingham in 1697 and the bridge fell down. So the bridge now standing was repaired or rebuilt in 1698. There is also a concrete bridge over the water for traffic, which in time of flood becomes a ford. *Whittle dean is a deep woody dell which stretches southwards & joins the Tyne east of Ovington. The waters of this dean (peculiarly soft & clear) are the most celebrated in the north of England for whitening linen cloth. Mr. William Newton's bleach green, situated on this stream at the confluence of the Tyne is known and famed throughout all these northern parts.* (Mackenzie 1825).

56. Welton Tower and Hall.

The Whittle Burn can be traced back to the present day Whittledean Water Works on either side of the Roman Wall near Welton Hall. There are other pleasant walks in this area along the river and across the fields as described in *Country Walks in East Tynedale* published by the local councils of the area.

There was a Dyehouse at Ovingham, and in 1828 William Bullock was the foreman. Both Thomas Bewick and George Stephenson had relatives who were dyers. One of Bewick's woodcuts is entitled the Dyers of Ovingham. Two men are carrying a large tub on a pole. Mabel Stephenson, George's mother, was daughter of an Ovingham dyer named Richard Carr. There were weavers in Ovingham, but one man, George Dobson, is described as a 'tidewaiter', and I wonder what he did.

The Tyne continued to provide an obstacle between Ovingham and Prudhoe until 20th December 1883, when a toll bridge was finally opened, taking the place of the ferry.

Along the road from Ovingham to Wylam can be seen the tall chimney of the Wylam Pumping Station. It was built in 1874—5 by the Newcastle & Gateshead Water Company to pump water from the Tyne, which was filtered and forced up to Horsley and the Company's reservoirs at Whittle Dean, joining the water of North Tyne, later to serve Newcastle. The aqueduct from Whittle can be seen from the road between High Barns and Harlow Hill.

Wylam

Looking at Wylam today, it is hard to believe what Mackenzie wrote in 1825. *Here is an extensive colliery belonging to Christopher Blackett Esq. in which a number of workmen are employed. The coal is worked on the south side of the Tyne, conveyed under the river and drawn up here; and from hence by locomotive engines by a railway to Lemington, a distance of above 5 miles. Each engine draws 10 waggons that carry 8 chaldrons of coals of 21⅓ tons, which is above 2 tons and one tenth to each waggon. Sometimes a dozen or more waggons are dragged by one engine. A stranger is struck with surprise & astonishment on seeing a locomotive engine moving majestically along the*

57. Wylam Road Bridge.

107

road at the rate of *4 or 5 miles an hour, drawing along 10 to 14 loaded waggons: and his surprise is increased on witnessing the extraordinary facility with which the engine is managed. The invention is a noble triumph of science. Here are also a number of cinder ovens in which the small coal is prepared for the use of manufactories. Wylam coal is chiefly consumed in steam engines, for which it is found well adapted. The village contains about 140 houses, including 3 public houses. Most of the inhabitants are engaged in the coal works.* He adds that Wylam once belonged to the Priory of Tynemouth.

One matter of interest is what may have been the first Tyne tunnel to convey coal beneath the water. There was no bridge, but eventually two railway lines and two stations — north and south of the river. The north line has been dismantled, but there is a plaque on the Station house on the south line to Benjamin Thompson, Engineer 1779—1867. He was born near Sheffield, and became an engineer, coal owner and ironmaster. In 1825 he became a Director of the Newcastle—Carlisle Railway, surveying the route, and later taking part in the construction in the years 1833—8. In 1835 he set up Wylam Bridge to link the village to the new railway. This Wylam Bridge was bought by the Northumberland County Council in 1936 and was freed from tolls. The piers were built in 1836 and originally supported a colliery waggonway. After extensive damage by floods in January 1957 the foundations of the piers were protected and two piers rebuilt. The superstructure was renewed and widened in 1960. The inn on the south side of the bridge is called the Boat House.

Railway Pioneers

In 1829 Benjamin Thompson guided the bill for the Newcastle and Carlisle Railway through the House of Commons. Local objections were about floods; in 1828 the river reached a depth of five feet above the proposed line. However, the bill passed the House and work was begun in 1830. By 1834 the line from Blaydon to Hexham was completed. The two earliest locomotives were Rapid (Stephenson) and Comet (Hawthorn). These were used for the opening ceremony of March 9th 1835, which was a great occasion. By 1836 it was extended to Haydon Bridge and Redheugh the other way. The other end of the line was being constructed from Carlisle, but it was not till June 18th 1838 that the gap was closed. In 1839 the extension was made to Newcastle with a bridge at Scotswood. Scandinavian timber could now be carried directly from Newcastle to Carlisle. There was much traffic in coal and lead. From 1840, cheap Sunday excursions by rail were begun, but the practice met with opposition from Sabbatarians. One preacher spoke of it as the quickest way to hell.

The Central Station in Newcastle, designed by Dobson, was not completed till 1850. On August 29th of that year it was opened by Queen Victoria and Prince Albert. The High Level Bridge linking Newcastle and Gateshead in 1849 required 5,000 tons of wrought iron supplied by Hawks, Crawshay & Co. of Gateshead and Losh, Wilson & Bell of Walker Ironworks. A roadway was ingeniously suspended beneath the railway, and both are still in service. The genius of Robert Stephenson was responsible for both this and the Royal Border Bridge which was completed in 1850.

58. Wylam Old Bridge.

The Newcastle and Carlisle Railway did not serve the north bank of the Tyne, and from 1871 there was a scheme for the Scotswood, Newburn and Wylam Railway. It was completed in 1876 with the construction of the magnificent Wylam bridge with a span of 240 feet. It consisted of one arch with the bridge floor suspended by vertical ties like the later Tyne Bridge. It cost £16,000 and its testing was severe. First, a locomotive with tender together weighing 61 tons made several crossings. Then another tank engine of 45 tons was added to the load, and finally 6 coupled locomotives with tenders weighing 350 tons in all were taken over several times at speed. The bridge did not falter and it still stands, serving a trackway on the riverside walk and preserved as a monument to the railway age in what might be considered its cradle. George Stephenson was born in a cottage along the old waggonway to the east of Wylam, but the family moved on to Newburn and others played a prominent part in the development of the steam locomotive.

Wylam now has a Railway Museum in the old school, and in the village it honours the Railway Pioneers with plaques. On a house near the Jubilee Field (1977) is one to Timothy Hackworth. He was born in Wylam near the Colliery Workshops in 1786. By 1807 he was blacksmith foreman and involved in the construction of Hedley's locomotives here. Hackworth became the residential engineer of the Stockton to Darlington Railway, completed in 1825. His locomotive Sans Pareil perfomed well at the Rainhill Trials, where Stephenson's Rocket was the winner. He had established his own workshops at Shildon, where he worked till his death in 1850.

William Hedley was born at Newburn in 1779 and went to school at Wylam. At the age of 22 he became viewer or manager of Walbottle Colliery and later of Wylam. During the French Wars horses became very expensive and Christopher Blackett, owner of the colliery at Wylam, turned to steam. He tried a Trevithick type of engine which failed. The problem was adhesion to the waggonway and the rack system proved unsatisfactory. Hedley considered the answer was a smooth

109

wheel on a smooth rail and began to experiment. He proved that his ideas were workable, and had a locomotive constructed which was nicknamed Puffing Billy after him. In due course his locomotive could be seen moving along the track pulling coal waggons. (Mackenzie). He may be considered to have constructed an early paddle steamer. In 1822 during a keelman's strike, he fitted a steam engine on to a barge to drive paddles and pull a line of keels to the waiting colliers. Sir Charles Parsons, who invented the steam turbine, lived for a time at Holeyn Hall not far away, and carried out some of his experiments at Ryton on the other side of Tyne. The Turbinia, the first ship to be powered by steam turbine, appeared unofficially at the Naval Review in 1897. Turbines were used in the production of a new form of power — electricity.

It might be mentioned here that during the construction of the Kielder Dam, British Railways had a contract to carry cement supplied by the Ribblesdale Cement Company from Clitheroe. The cement was carried by 15 waggon trains from Clitheroe to Carlisle and then to Hexham, where it was transferred to road lorries. 10,000 tons of cement were carried each year (1977-1980).

In medieval times Wylam belonged to the Prior of Tynemouth and there was a Monk's House here. The tenants were expected to do carting services — carrying goods each way. The Monk's House was destroyed by the Scots, but was rebuilt and later embodied in Wylam Hall. With the Dissolution of the Monasteries, these lands came into the hands of the Crown. John Swinburne, who leased them, had a fishery, a coal mine and a dovecote. A dovecote, like a fishery, deerpark or warren, was a privilege and helped to provide fresh food.

There are riverside walks from Wylam on the north side to Newburn and on the south side to Ryton in County Durham. From Wylam the Tyne is the boundary between the two counties, previously it was the Stanley Burn and Derwent river.

Wylam Close House

The walk along the north bank passes a fishpond, where anyone can fish for rainbow trout, and beyond is Stephenson's cottage. From here can be seen higher in wooded surroundings Wylam Close House. The land belonged in medieval times to the Turpins, then the Reads and the Bewickes. The Bewickes were Merchant Adventurers of Newcastle, and in 1779 this very fine hall was built in classical style. It has a five bay front of two and a half storeys having a slight three bay projection with pediment. The doorway has Tuscan columns to support the door head. The other fronts have five bays and there is a conservatory of five bays with Tuscan columns to the north west. Close House is now used as the sports centre for the University of Newcastle and it includes the Bewicke Restaurant and Bar. From the south front are magnificent views of the Tyne Valley, where the river and railways run.

Along the north bank of the river below Heddon on the Wall is an area called Ryton Island, part of Ryton parish and County Durham. The island remained until the river changed its course. Here is the tidal limit, and also the limit of the authority of the Port of Newcastle. There was no bridge but a ferry. The deepening of the river and the construction of embankments helped the changes. The work was done by the Tyne Improvement Commission. A boundary stone here carried the date 1785, and it is called the Kissing Stone. The reason is that on Ascension Day for the river parade and beating the bounds, the Mayor's ceremonial barge reached this spot. At one time the Mayor greeted a village maiden with a kiss and so the stone got its name.

Heddon

Heddon village is hardly a mile above the river, but the climb is steep and when the height is reached the views are extensive. Here the Hexham road diverges from the Military Road, which followed the line of the Roman Wall, used for building material. Some 100 yards of wall east of Heddon which escaped, have been exposed and can be inspected. The foundations were 10½ feet in width on which were erected the 'broad' wall, 9½ feet wide still standing several courses high. The vallum can be seen on the hill further to the east. In 1752 a number of boxes containing Roman coins were discovered but not properly recorded.

59. Heddon-on-the-Wall Church.

Stone from the Roman Wall was taken to build the Church of St Andrew at Heddon. A church existed there in Anglo Saxon times, and indications are that it consisted of nave, chancel and apse. The same layout was used in the Norman period, and the church measures 51½ feet by 20 feet for the nave, chancel 16 feet long, choir 17 feet long and both 13½ feet wide. The apse has disappeared. The rounded Norman arch still stands between chancel and choir. The chancel roof is rib vaulted like Warkworth and of the same period. Outside the church the south east corner of the nave shows the large quoin stones of the Saxon church. In the late twelfth century the north aisle was added, as was the south aisle in the thirteenth century. There is a neat bell cote at the west end of the church.

This area of the Tyne was essentially a coal mining area and there were collieries at Heddon. Here we have a reminder of the French Revolution. Atrocities

111

committed by the revolutionaries, caused clergy and others to flee the country. They were called 'emigres' and homes had to be found for them. A row of mining cottages was empty east of Heddon — 11 houses, two storeys high, provided room for 38 refugees. This was called Frenchman's Row, and one house was later rebuilt as an inn and called the Royal French Arms. Citizen Marat, prominent in Paris during the Reign of Terror and murdered in his bath, once walked the streets of Newcastle and worked as a 'doctor' or horse doctor, in the Tyne area.

Newburn

Eastwards from Heddon and nearer the river is Newburn, strictly New 'Burh', since it was a Saxon town of considerable importance. In Norman times here in 1067 Copsi, the Earl of Northumberland, was burnt in the church. The fine strong square tower of the church was built after this date. The church is dedicated to St Michael, principal fighter of the heavenly host and appropriately too since Newburn has seen a number of battles. It is interesting that the advowson of the church was granted to the Bishop of Carlisle with whom it remained till 1882 when the Bishopric of Newcastle was created. The Church consists of a nave of four bays with north and south aisles. There were north and south transeptal chapels and a chancel. The tower, later embodied in the aisles, was built in the early twelfth century with the nave. The north aisle was built c. 1175 with round columns and large square capitals. The south aisle was early thirteenth century with alternate round and octagonal pillars.

The tower measures 14 feet by 15 feet internally and 21 feet by 22 feet externally. The west door was blocked and the lower windows were narrow slits, but widely splayed. At the belfry stage there were double round headed openings with a shaft between and within a round arch. There is possibly pre-Norman stonework and Roman stone was used. The church has been much restored, but the chancel with lancet windows retains much thirteenth century work. There is a round headed arch between tower and nave. The measurements of the nave are 45 feet by 17½ feet internally, chancel 41½ feet by 17½ feet. The full width is 22 feet and the transepts add about 20 feet square on each side.

Entry is by a porch on the south side. The most important monumental slab within is that of Sir John Delaval who died on 12th August 1652 in Cromwell's time. Cromwell had crossed the Tyne here in 1651 during his Scottish campaign.

Newburn was important because of its fords which provided river crossings at the tidal limit, and the river was navigable to this point. there were three known fords — the Romans certainly crossed here as did the Scots on numerous occasions. Spring tides were the deepest, when the 'stanners' were liable to flooding. In 1732 it is recorded that Newburn sands were used for horse racing.

On 28th August 1640 Newburn was the site of a disgraceful defeat of the troops of Charles I by the Scots under General Lesley. The Scots had a much stronger army and had cannon, some of which were said to be placed on the church tower. These covered the crossing and the Royalist troops were forced to retreat with heavy losses. Many skeletons were found in excavating a quarry in 1897, together with cannon balls and other relics of war. The Scots used the same fords in 1643/4 before the siege of Newcastle. The Newburn ford was to the west, the Kelshaw ford on the east side of the town and the Riding ford was between them. They could only be used on ebb tide.

Newburn Hall was a tower to which a sixteenth century house was added. The Manor House was demolished in 1909. George Stephenson lived for a time at Newburn and both his marriages are in the church records. This was very much a mining and railway place. There was the Duke Pit, the Blucher Pit and King Pit at Newburn and the North Walbottle Pit and the Coronation Pit nearby.

When Newburn was acquired by the Percies in 1367, it had a dovecot, two water mills, a brewery, a fishery, a coal mine and a quarry for stone slates. In 1613 it was reported that no woods of any value were left — they had been used for providing timber for coal pits and the building of staiths. In 1623 three mills are mentioned. The Directory of 1828 recorded that Newburn had *many extensive ironworks: coal staiths, brick & tile yards & chemical works: also a crown glass house, 2 corn mills, a paper mill & an extensive coal mine.*

J. Spenser & Sons manufactured files, springs and material for mines and railways. The work force was much increased and many more houses were built. Newburn had continuous water transport and railway. In 1828 the inn was the Boat House, and a ferryboat was still used. The iron bridge over the Tyne was built in 1894, at a time when the U.D. Council was established. The steel works continued to be prosperous until after the War of 1914-18. Depression followed and they were closed in 1924.

There were a number of fisheries at Newburn, connected with Finchale and Hexham Priories, and after the Dissolution these were granted to other persons. The Duke of Northumberland had two and between 1871 and 1883 there was much embanking, straightening and dredging by the Tyne Improvement Commission. A sharp bend called the Crook was cut off. Newburn was one of the principal salmon fisheries, and on June 12th 1755, more than 2,400 fish were taken. On 20th June 1758 more than 2,000 were netted. Thomas Bewick was a keen fisherman and wrote - *Every improper weir or dam that obstructs this (the passage of fish) ought to be thrown down.* Moreover *The filth of manufacturers & other refuse should be led away & laid on the land; it would be of great value to the farmer.* His advice was not heeded and pollution has become a perennial problem, though late in our own times some action is being taken, and more salmon return to the river.

Industrial Tyne

By the end of the Napoleonic Wars (1815), the Tyne was wearing the black and busy look of an industrial region. *From Lemington to Shields its banks were lined not only with collieries, but factories, foundries and forges: with glass houses, breweries & refineries: with chemical works & shipbuilding yards.*

On the south side of the river at Swalwell and Winlaton were the Crowley ironworks, seen by Arthur Young. Isaac Cookson had ironworks at Derwentcote. At Blaydon was a lead refinery and flint mill with a large pottery at St. Anthony's. At Derwenthaugh there were coal tar ovens and coke manufacturing plant. At Lemington on the north side was established an ironworks in 1797, and here was the Crown Glass House of the Northumberland Glass Company. There were two coal staiths, served by waggonways. A large glass making cone is still a feature of the landscape, but the round shot tower, 175 feet high, at Elswick has disappeared.

Ryton

Across the river from Newburn is Ryton. Palmer who approached by train, wrote *From the din and smoke of neighbouring industries, Ryton must be a pleasant retreat.*

The pathway from the station passed through the trees to the village green, where stood the cross. The church, seen from below, is rather different from the majority of churches in the North east, having a tall spire, which rises attractively through the trees. In 1802 the village was *flourishing & containing many handsome buildings inhabited by opulent families.*

The most impressive is Ryton Grove, dated 1742 by rainwater heads. It is built of brick with stone dressings and central bay windows.

Another house with attractive gardens was the Rectory which has a nine bay Georgian front, hiding the earlier building of the late sixteenth or early seventeenth century. There are other attractive houses, which make it one of the most delightful villages of Tyneside.

The Church is dedicated to the Holy Cross, and consists of a strong west tower, broached with a lead covered spire. It has a wide nave with columns both round and octagonal. The aisles are 'engaged', that is they extend to the west wall of the tower as at Newburn. The long chancel has lancet windows, and a remarkable feature is the seventeenth century woodwork of the Cosin period. This is the chancel screen with flamboyant tracery and stalls of the same period. The altar rails have carved sixteenth century figures. Monuments include a slab from the tomb of Bernard Gilpin from Houghton le Spring, and two brasses of the Bunny family. Francis Bunny, who was Rector 1578-1617 *having buried here his four sons & his daughter at York, hastened to heaven after them.*

The Revd. Thomas Secker left the village in 1735, later to become the Archbishop of Canterbury. There is a monument of a thirteenth century clergyman, carved from Frosterley marble. He is shown carrying a book.

Ryton is a holiday haunt and place for visitors, with 54 acres of riverside common called Ryton Willows. It is often busy with picnickers and the river lively with boats. The area is still well wooded.

114

description of Dante's Inferno with terrible wailings. Some thought that the end of the world had come, and called upon God for mercy. Many persons were laid out dead and others taken to hospital.

In Gateshead things were worse with falling masonry and burning material filling the narrow streets. The number of victims was very difficult to estimate. More warehouses and houses were destroyed, but in Newcastle, though there were not so many casualties, the fire seemed to spread more extensively both northwards and eastwards, helped by the wind and the nature of the housing, being very crowded. By 6 a.m. the fire had spread 120 yards along the Quayside, up the chares and to Butcher Bank. On both sides of the river the fires were most difficult to control, though engines came from as far as Durham and Berwick. It was not until the 8th that the fires were quenched and the debris could be searched for bodies. Often they were quite consumed and identification came from personal items. John Dobson's son was identified from a bunch of keys, Thomas Sharp from a gold watch and two dog whistles, a Mr Harrison from a cigar case, and others not at all.

When the inquest was held, it was asserted that gunpowder had been stored in the warehouse, but experts considered that the chemicals that were housed there, could have the explosive effect. The result was that there was vast destruction of property on both sides of the river. A great deal of rebuilding was necessary on the Quayside and the adjoining streets. At St Mary's Church Gateshead, there was a stone inscribed *This stone with burning timber and red hot iron bars were blown onto the roof & into the church by the explosion in Hillgate October 6th 1854. Weight of the largest stone about 6 cwt.*

In recent years St Mary's Church, which became redundant, has again suffered from the effects of fire and now stands blackened with windows boarded.

On the Quayside now demolition goes on apace, but this is for the purpose of redeveloping the river bank. Some buildings from the rebuilding of 1854 have gone the way of their predecessors, and there is much change upon both banks of the Tyne. History records many unusual happenings here.

In 1856 September 28th, *The main damage on both sides of the Tyne was the produce in the fields, in many of which the stooks were swept down & the sheaves washed about & in many cases, to such an extent was it brought down the river that at one time the Tyne, opposite Newcastle Quay, was covered with floating corn.*

In January 1768 at the Sandhill, there was a bull baiting of two bulls. In the excitement a soldier got too near and was gored by one of the bulls, dying from his wounds.

The winter of 1739—40 was very harsh and the Tyne was frozen over for many weeks. It was at first a source of fun and tents were set up on the ice, but there was soon a shortage of food. The coal trade came to a stand-still and wages were not paid. Some men were set on to cut the ice. The Mayor and magistrates had been considering the sale of a ship-load of grain, but nothing was done and the mob attacked the Guildhall. The windows were smashed, records destroyed and £1000 in cash was taken. After this the mob broke into the granaries and helped themselves to the corn.

In May 1742 John Wesley came to Newcastle and went with John Taylor to the

Sandgate 'the poorest and most contemptible part of the town'. It was Sunday and they began to sing a psalm. A few people came to see at first, but before he finished preaching a great crowd gathered. In the afternoon he preached again to another crowd, and that same year the first stone of Orphan House was laid — the second Methodist chapel to be built in England. Newcastle was a favourite town to him and he came many times to stay.

63. Armstrong's Swing Bridge, Newcastle.

On the Quayside below what was the Milk Market, is a tall standing obelisk, the John Wesley Centenary Memorial erected in 1891, a hundred years after his death. The monument provided a supply of water. Methodism had a great influence on the lives of miners and keelmen. The area eastwards along the river was called the Sandgate, again because of the sandy deposits of the river, and it was built upon. Bourne wrote that here, like the Quayside there were a lot of narrow streets, and this was the area where many of the keelmen lived. The numerous chares became overcrowded and there was little care for sanitation, so that there were outbreaks of cholera and typhus. Late in the nineteenth century these slums were cleared and replaced by warehouses and factories like Thomas Hedleys. Hedleys were the makers of the famous 'Fairy' soap, and have become part of the Proctcor and Gamble empire, a reminder of the great Tyneside chemical industry. In turn many of these buildings have been demolished and are awaiting development. We are reminded of the popular Tyneside song called the 'Keel Row', sung when we did not know what it was about. i.e.(carrying coal on the Tyne).

> As I came thro' Sandgate,
> Thro' Sandgate, thro' Sandgate,
> As I came thro' Sandgate,
> I heard a lassie sing.
> O weel may the keel row,
> The keel row, the keel row,

to the north of the Walls as an open space, in spite of approaches by urban developers. Here can still be seen the cattle grazing as they did in medieval times. In 1653 there was a neatherd to look after the cattle with four assistants. Their duties were in the morning, after milking, to blow their horns through the streets as a signal to owners to bring out their cows to be driven to the Town Moor for grazing.

Cattle and Horse Fairs were held on the Town Moor, which in 1773, by Act of Parliament, became the property of the Corporation with the right to lease the land. Each freemen or his widow had the right to herbage for two milch cows for ever.

Horse Races were held on the Town Moor, and the tradition continues with the Race Week Hoppings. The Racecourse is now at Gosforth Park.

The Joicey Museum contains many more illustations of Newcastle's history — the Flood of 1771 and a model of the bridge that was destroyed. There are scenes of the Great Fire, but also more pleasant scenes. There is a series of pictures by Henry Parker, who painted many of people and places in the area. He did much to promote the arts in Newcastle. One room provides information about the Shotley Bridge swordmakers, with examples of their craft. They were taken over by William Cotesworth, and their products were much in demand at the time of the Jacobite Rebellions of 1715 and 1745. The craft of blade making was carried on by Wilkinsons. On display also are a collection of sporting guns, and the old weights and measures of the town, used from 1824 by the trading inspectorate. The old Armoury from Alnwick Castle has been reconstructed in the old tower and shows how the weapons were made. Beneath is a prison cell, and altogether the visitor is provided with a fascinating picture of Newcastle's past.

71. Holy Jesus Hospital, now the Joicey Museum.

Brand gives a description of the fountain there.

The public fountains, which at Newcastle are of a particular construction having each a small square reservoir before them for retaining the water for the use of horses, or for common domestic purposes, are called 'Pants'.

Horses, toiling up the steep streets and chares, would often need a drink.

The Church of All Saints next calls for attention. It is one of the most attractive buildings of the city, and from it there are exciting views over the river and the quayside. It was in Henry Bourne's time the Church of All Hallows, a large medieval structure which fell into disrepair. In 1788 it was decided to demolish it and build anew in an entirely different style. The only ancient features are the gravestones of many Newcastle worthies, still etched with the smoke of coal. The finest monument, the brass of Roger Thornton, has been transferred to the Cathedral — high on the wall and not as originally on a table tomb. It must be one of the finest brasses in the country, and a plastic replica should be made for the benefit of brass rubbers and the profit of the church — it is unique. Thornton was Newcastle's 'Dick Whittington'. An old rhyme about him ran—

At the West Gate cam' Thornton in,
With hop, a halfpenny and a lamb's skin.

He became 'wonderous rich' and from 1400 he was eight times Mayor and three times MP. He had helped in the building of both St Nicholas and All Hallows Churches. In 1430 he was buried in the latter.

The design for the new church of All Saints was submitted by David Stephenson (1756—1818), and this was his masterpiece. John Dobson was a pupil of his and admired the classical style. The church stands on an elevated site above the river, and was even more outstanding before the railway viaduct was constructed. It is approached from the Quayside by a flight of steps, leading to a four columned portico. Above this the tower rises in several stages and styles — square and octagonal, plain and columned to a slender spire on top. The round top stone is 202 feet from the base of the church and when it was completed in 1796, John Burdkin, a Gateshead barber, stood on his head on it. His son, not to be outdone, repeated the performance in 1816. The church was consecrated by the Bishop of Durham, and the opening service was conducted by the Reverend Hugh Moises, formerly headmaster of the Royal Grammar School, and teacher of Collingwood and the brothers Scott.

The interior is surprising. The porch leads to the vestibule and the right is the vestry, on the left the Lady Chapel. Beyond these the assembly area for the congregation is circular in shape, like the Pantheon in Rome. There are apses on the east and west sides directly opposite each other. The east side had the altar, pulpit and rostrum. The seating is circular and there is also a gallery.

With changes in Newcastle, the population of the area was greatly diminished and the Church was closed in 1960. As a Grade 1 listed building it had to be saved and was purchased by the City Council. It was eventually converted into an urban studies centre under the control of Town Teacher Limited, an organisation directly involved in heritage and environmental education. Town Trails are provided and useful booklets on buildings and other features. Various community activities take place there and it is daily open to visitors, an excellent place from which to explore the city. (1991 Town Teacher has ended).

72. All Saint's Church, Newcastle.

The Castle

Since 1882 Newcastle has become a bishopric and St Nicholas Church has become the Cathedral. The Castle stands between it and All Saints, and the railway passes between the Castle Keep and the Black Gate, the medieval entrance to the Castle precinct. The ravine of the Lort Burn divides All Saints from the Castle, and it means a descent to the Side and up Dean Street to the Black Gate. The Dog Loup (Leap) Stairs are out of commission at the time of writing.

The Black Gate was built in the thirteenth century to protect the northern approach to the Castle. The other sides were protected by the river and the ravines of two burns, so that the site was roughly triangular in shape.

The original motte and bailey castle of earth and timber was built in the reign of William I (1080), by his son Robert Curthose (short legs). It had defensive ramparts, but was not sufficiently strong, so that the castle was rebuilt in the reign of Henry II in the years 1172-1177. It was the work of Maurice the Engineer, who constructed Dover Castle, and cost £911 10s. 9d. The Keep is considered to be one of the finest in the country and is the true symbol of Newcastle. It measures 62 feet by 56 feet at the base, and the battlements, restored by Dobson, stand more than 80 feet high. This height is not realized on the ground on account of the

141

railway viaduct cutting across the site, and the stonework was encrusted with coal smoke. The blackness is gradually dying away.

73. Newcastle Castle and the Moot Hall.

King John built a shell keep on the old motte, but this, called the 'old tower', and a later hall have disappeared. The keep has a broad plinth or base, tall buttresses and a projecting corner turrets. The doors and windows are round arched. The approach is by a forework which once had three towers, but only the middle and upper remain. The stair passes under a vaulted passage to the second floor where the entrance portal is. This structure added greatly to the strength of the place — the entrance was covered by three towers and the roof of the keep. The constable's room was in the upper tower, and he controlled the entry to the King's Hall. There was a number of small chambers within the thickness of the walls, including the King's Chamber. In another vaulted room is the well shaft which is 99 feet deep. The garderobes or latrines were within the thickness of the walls, and the shafts were covered by a thick buttress on the outside.

The first floor apartments, which had to be entered from the second floor, included the Queen's Chamber, within the thickness of the north wall, the opposite to the King's on the floor above. He would have a fine view of the river and the bridge. These apartments would appear much lighter than they seem now, because they would be decorated and there would be no other buildings to reduce the light. The placing of the King's and Queen's Chambers in different walls was to prevent the weakening of the structure.

Continuing down the spiral stair, the basement is reached. This is a vaulted cellar, dry and fireproof, within the thickest part of the walls. There is a central pillar from which eight semi-circular ribs spring to the corners and mid walls. In one corner was a secure prison. Water was brought down by a pipe in the central pillar. In the forebuilding is the Norman chapel — the nave has two bays and the chancel one. The arches are decorated with Norman zig-zag and other patterns. The stairways are complicated, and within the walls near roof level were galleries

142

to help the mobility of the defenders. Originally members of the garrison would have lodgings in the garret with a high pitched roof. Later the level of the upper storey was raised with a flat roof. This was covered with lead, laid on a bed of sand to make the roof fireproof from flaming missiles. The Keep retains items of Newcastle's history, and the Black Gate is a museum. The bag-pipe collection has been moved from here to the Chantry Museum at Morpeth.

The Black Gate is, like the gatehouse at Warkworth, a thirteenth century addition to strengthen the castle. It consisted of a vaulted passage with a semi-circular tower on each side, two storeys of which survive. It had a drawbridge (now fixed) over the ditch, a portcullis and a wooden gate. Once through here, there were more defences with ditch and drawbridge.

The Heron pit was a prison beneath another building, named after a constable. The gatehouse was restored into a house with brick structure and occupied by a man named Black, hence its name.

The Castle area tended to deteriorate as a royal building that was not maintained, and it was let by James I. Being outside the jurisdiction of the town, trade regulations could be evaded. Later the area was developed by the construction of the Moot Hall 1810-1812 by William Stokoe, a fine building of Greek classical style. The County Hall was built close to the Castle in 1910. Near the Moot Hall a length of the curtain wall of the Castle has been excavated and restored. The stairs lead through the south postern gate. Both the Keep and Black Gate were taken over by the Newcastle Council and restored. They are leased to the Society of Antiquaries of Newcastle and open to the public.

74. St Nicholas Cathedral from the Quayside.

A short distance from the Black Gate is St Nicholas Church, now the Cathedral. Its architecture is mainly of the fourteenth and fifteenth centuries, succeeding earlier constructions. The outstanding feature is the remarkable west tower with its spire. The square tower has corner buttresses and rises to battlements with pinnacles. From these, flying buttresses lend support to the so-called Scottish Crown. This spire consists of a smaller lantern with pinnacles and buttresses. It is

143

considered to be the finest of its kind, and rises to a height of 193½ feet. Robert Rhodes, a wealthy customs official, was responsible for its construction. During the siege of Newcastle 1644, when General Lesley threatened to batter it, Sir John Marley put Scottish prisoners there. The attack was not made and the church was saved. Later Cromwell kept Scottish prisoners in the nave.

The font dates from the Rhodes period and has a very elaborate wooden cover much in keeping with the spire. It saw many notable baptisms, and the church received important burials and monuments. Special mention might be made of the Maddison monument c.1635, and again the brass of Roger Thornton.

Two other interesting medieval churches are those of St John and St Andrew. The remains of the northern part of the Town Wall passes through St Andrew's churchyard, and from here it is possible to follow the best stretch of the Wall, which stands to 20 feet high. The towers still standing are the Ever Tower, the Morden Tower, the Heber Tower and the Durham Tower. Each projects as a semi-circle from the Wall. The ditch is visible beyond the Wall and within the Wall at the western corner is the *Blackfriars*.

It was founded in the thirteenth century by the Dominican Friars and dissolved in the reign of Henry VIII. The premises were taken over by nine Craft Guilds who used them for their meetings. It fell into disrepair, but has been restored by the City Council and made into the crafts centre with a restaurant and an exhibition of Newcastle's history. The area was excavated to reveal the plan of the church, and some of the finds are on display.

The Civil War witnessed the battering of the Town Walls, and they were later broken down to allow for industrial expansion and increasing population.

In 1750 it was 20,000 and in 1851 had reached 88,000. By 1911 it had passed 250,000. The villages on either side were taken over and the town expanded rapidly to the north.

An early development was the building of Eldon Square 1824-6. Named after the Lord Chancellor, it was designed by John Dobson and built by Richard Grainger. In recent years it has developed into a very large shopping complex. In 1829 Thomas Oliver was responsible for the construction of Leazes Terrace, a very fine range of classical buildings overlooking Leazes Park and, at the present day St James' Football Ground. Dobson and Grainger together with John Clayton, Town Clerk, were responsible for the planned development of central Newcastle. The layout was conditioned by the medieval streets, but it is considered to be one of the finest in the country. The main streets were Grainger Street with the Grainger Market and Grey Street with its curve of splendid buildings which include the Theatre Royal. Grey's Column provides a feature that can be viewed from several directions. Clayton gave his name to another street, but only recently has the name of John Dobson been given to a street, and his Central Station is still regarded as a masterpiece. Opposite and in contrast is St Mary's Catholic Cathedral with its tall spire.

For public buildings, the Assembly Rooms were built in Westgate Road by William Newton (1774-6). The Town Hall and Corn Exchange were built by John Johnson in St Nicholas Square 1858-63. The City Hall came in 1928 and in 1968 there was a complete change to the Civic Centre at the Haymarket near St. Thomas's Church. In this area too the University has developed remarkably and the old Armstrong College is only a small part. Newcastle can also boast a large Polytechnic College.

Much more could be added but special attention has to be called to the Central Library and the Laing Art Gallery off New Bridge Street as well as the Museum of

144

Science and Engineering and the Archives Department in Blandford Square. All provide information and enlightment.

On Claremont Road is a rare relic — the timber framed tower of a windmill built by Smeaton in 1786. Here, too, might be mentioned the Ouseburn, another tributary of the waters of Tyne. It begins in the Callerton area south of Ponteland and ignores the Pont, flowing to Woolsington and Gosforth where it continues under the medieval Salter's Bridge. It passes Mr Brandling's Gosforth House, build by Paine 1755-64, and damaged by suffragettes in 1914. This is now the Race Course area. The stream continues into Jesmond Dene, a place of great beauty. In the last century here lived Sir William Armstrong, and his associates Charles Mitchell and Sir Andrew Noble in their fine houses. The Ouseburn makes its way to the Tyne under its own bridges — the viaduct built in 1868 of timber, then of iron, and the Byker Bridge, showing the fascinating difference in levels. The area at the mouth of the Ouseburn was famed for its glassworks. There were also shipyards, engine works, potteries, roperies, soapworks, lead-smelting and chemical works.

In 1887 an Exhibition was held on the Town Moor to commemorate Queen Victoria's Diamond Jubilee. What had been a reservoir to supply water to Newcastle was converted into a lake. It had been fed from 1805 by water from an underground stream at Coxlodge Colliery, pumped by a windmill.

In 1929 The North East Coast Exhibition was held here to *display to the World the marvellous products of modern science and business organization, its scope is as extensive as the British Empire itself* . . .

The main buildings were the Palace of Engineering, the Palace of Industry, the Palace of Arts, a Festival Hall, a Garden Club and other features. It was opened by the Prince of Wales on May 14th, 1929. Exhibits included Sir Charles Parson's 'Turbinia', Malcolm Campbell's 'Bluebird', and the 'Supermarine 56 Seaplane'. There were all kinds of displays, games and entertainment. By October 29th, when it closed, 4,373,138 people had attended and a small profit was gained. The buildings were dismantled except the Palace of Arts which became the Museum of Science and Engineering. *'Turbinia' stayed there, and the bridge over the lake was also retained.*

75. St Mary's Church, Gateshead.

145

Chapter Seven. South of the Tyne

Gateshead

In 1990 on the other side of the Tyne, the Metro Shopping Centre is flourishing and a 200 acre site was provided for a National Garden Festival. It has been said that Gateshead is the place for the finest view of Newcastle, but now Gateshead has shown that much can be admired on the south bank. The river and the bridges are as much the concern of Gateshead as of Newcastle.

There is some argument about the origin of the name 'Gateshead'. One version is that it means 'The end of the street'. The other, on the authority of the Venerable Bede, is that it was called *'Caput Caprae'*, meaning 'goat's head'. The heraldry of the town gives a goat's head above the castle gate with the motto — *Caput inter nubila condit* — 'the head rises up among the clouds'. It is only in recent years, however, that Gateshead has high-rise buildings. The churches had no towers like the churches and castle of Newcastle. It was, however, part of the principality of the Bishop of Durham, who granted a charter. The town was governed by the 24, until 1835 when reform provided a Mayor and Corporation and a Member of Parliament. In 1889 Gateshead became a County Borough.

The town had to resist Newcastle's desire for control. In 1553, in Edward VI's reign, Gateshead was annexed and to annoy the Bishop of Durham, it was proposed to set up a Bishopric of Newcastle. Queen Mary gave Gateshead back its freedom, and another attempt in Elizabeth's reign at a Newcastle take-over failed. Yet Newcastle continued to exercise considerable control of river traffic and trade in coal. The Hostmen's Company had the sole right to trade in coal and grindstones shipped from the Tyne (1600).

Gateshead has tended not to keep its old buildings. St Mary's Church, fired in 1080, was rebuilt and suffered again in the fire of 1854. It was largely rebuilt by Dobson, whose son was lost in the conflagration. Wailes provided the glass for the East window. Again, after becoming redundant with the shift of population, it has suffered from fire and its future is in doubt. It had part of a pre-conquest cross and some fine woodwork. Here were buried Timothy Tyzack and his wife, and Henzells who were glass makers. Robert Trollope was also buried here.

Holy Trinity Church has become the Trinity Community Centre. Its south aisle is the thirteenth century Chapel of St Edmund, restored by Dobson. It was connected with a medieval hospital and William Riddell built Gateshead House on part of the site. It was later owned by the Claverings of Callaly, who were Catholics, and members of both families are buried here. In 1611 the hospital was refounded as King James's Hospital. Gateshead House was burnt by a riotous mob in 1746. In 1832 the Revd. John Collinson had an obelisk erected as a memorial to 222 victims of the cholera epidemic. In 1831 the census reported that 3,429 families lived in 2,197 houses in Gateshead. The houses of Pipewellgate and Hillgate were badly affected with damp because of lack of drainage. Pipewellgate, 300 yards in length had a population of 2,040, many living in cellars. There were only three privies and no drainage, since it had been considered that none was needed on a steep slope. In 1849 there were 186 more victims of cholera. Problems of sanitation and health took a long time to solve. The fire of 1854 cleared some of the Hillgate property.

In 1831 Thomas Oliver descending from Windmill Hills to Redheugh listed the industries near the river — Paper Mill, Mr Sowerby's Flint Glass House, Iron Works, Gas Works and Lime Kilns.

On entering Pipewellgate, a long narrow dirty street, he found a Whiting and Colour Manufactory, a Glue Factory, a Foundry and Blacking Factory, a Skinnery and the Flint Glass Works of Joseph Price. There were also a number of clay pipe makers. Beyond the bridge at Hillgate was a ferry landing and boat builders yard. At New Greenwich were a Ropery and Ironworks. Then came the Iron Works of Messrs. Wm. Hawks, another Ropery, Paper Mill and the Tyne Glass Company's Works. On the Salt Meadows were an Oil Yard, Cinder Ovens, a Ballast Quay, a Chemical Factory, a Shipbuilding Yard, Colliery, Staiths and Spouts.

On July 16th 1833 it was reported —

A most magnificent brick built chimney having been completed by Mr. Livingston at the alkali works of Anthony Clapham Esq., Friar's Goose, on the Tyne, a little below Newcastle, Mr. Clapham on the above day entertained a party of friends with a sumptuous repast at the bottom of that chimney, to the great delight of his friends, who expressed their surprise & astonishment at this stupendous work of art. It was then the highest chimney in England, being 263 feet from the base, exceeding the height of Muspratt's famous chimney at Liverpool by 69 feet. It is 27 feet in diameter at the base & 7 feet at the top. It contains upwards of half a million bricks & is computed to weigh nearly 2000 tons. So Gateshead could claim at least one better than Newcastle.

In 1858 these premises were bought by Mr Williamson of Jarrow Alkali Works for £14,050.

A century later Pevsner wrote: *Pumping Engine House, Friar's Goose, E. of the town near the riverside. Built c.1820 to pump water from Tyne Main Colliery. Its derelict remains are surrounded by the now landscaped alkali waste heaps of Gateshead's vanished chemical works.*

In 1747 William Hawks, a foreman blacksmith, at Crowley's Swalwell Works, started his ironworks using iron waste, brought in as ballast, to make bar iron and steel, using a watermill to work hammers. His son expanded the industry even having a rolling mill at Bedlington. He also used steam power, and gained government contracts during the French Wars, making cannon, mortars and cannon balls. His works also produced anchors, chains, bolts, spades, picks and other tools at Bottlebank, Gateshead. Works and warehouses took the names of New Woolwich and New Deptford. They later combined with Crawshay and Stanley in 1838 for a London Branch, and in 1843 for the Gateshead branch. Employing 843 men and 157 youths, it was the largest ironworks on Tyneside. In 1844 the first Nasmyth steam hammer was set up in the North East. Hawks provided 5050 tons of iron for the High Level Bridge, and George Hawks drove the last key into place, 7th June 1849. For some years Hawks flourished, but rivals like Armstrong were rising, and in 1889 the firm closed. The plant and tools were sold. Time came for Armstrongs too, and they were taken over by Vickers in 1938, but Vickers continues to the present day.

From 1840 Christian Allhusen developed Alkali Works on the south shore. It became a very large concern and was taken over by the United Alkali Company in 1891, which also amalgamated with Friar's Goose Works. United Alkali was taken over by I.C.I. in 1926. In process of time all transferred to Billingham. The spoil

147

heaps, however, have been used for agricultural lime, and land recovered from the 'Great Heap' was included in the East Gateshead Riverside Park, developed from 1960.

George Hawks was the first Mayor of Gateshead and Allhusen was a member of the Council. After the Fire of 1854, it was proposed to form a Corporation Quay at Hillgate. It proved difficult to raise the money, and the N.E. Railway was unwilling to finance rail links, so it was not successful and became a financial embarrassment. Newcastle Quay was congested with traffic at the same time and was profitable.

While Newcastle claimed lordship of the river with its barge procession, Gateshead citizens used to beat their own bounds, with two constables and two pipers playing the 'Keel Row'. They began at St. Mary's Church and went on to the blue stone part way across the Tyne Bridge. The bells would ring and guns fire as they went along to Friar's Goose and took the boat back for dinner at the Black Bull.

'The Hoppings' of Gateshead were held on the Windmill Hills, where there was for years a battery of windmills with their sails turning. In 1829 races included what was called a hat run for men and another for boys, 'a cheese run for men tied up in sacks, and a pound of tobacco to be "grinned" for through a horse's collar.' There was another prize of tobacco for the winner of the wrestlings.

The windmills gradually closed down and were demolished — the last one in 1927. In 1644 cannons placed on Windmill Hills were used by the Parliamentarians to bombard the walls of Newcastle and enforce surrender.

Park House, the manor house of Gateshead, was at one time considered to be the 'Gateshead Hall' of Charlotte Bronte's Jane Eyre, but this is no longer accepted. However there was named a Jane Eyre Terrace, Bronte Street and Shirley Street. The house has figured in a life of a different kind — that of 'Black William' Cotesworth, a great entrepreneur in local industry. The Cotesworth Papers were rescued from salvage in the Second World War and Professor Hughes made use of them in his work on *North Country Life in the C18th.*

Cotesworth was born in 1668, son of yeoman farmer in Teesdale. In 1682 he was bound apprentice to Robert Sutton of Gateshead, a tallow and corn chandler, who had a foul smelling shop on Bottle Bank where animal fat was rendered. Cotesworth soon rose to partnership with Sutton's son, and in 1705 set up his own. He married well — Hannah, daughter of William Ramsey, a Newcastle goldsmith. Candles were used locally for lighting, but he developed a London market. He traded in grindstones, lead, glass bottles and Shotley swords. Much he exported to the continent and imported flax, hemp and whalebone. He gained control of South Shields Salt pans and supplied the government. The coal trade brought him more wealth and he exploited 'way leaves'. Coalowners had to pay to use waggonways to the river. He bought and leased considerable estate. In 1715 he was a government agent against the rebels, to his profit. When he died in 1726, he was wealthy but not popular.

Park House was rebuilt by him in 1723, and enlarged by his son-in-law, Henry Ellison. The Ellisons lived here till 1825, when it was leased to various industrialists. In 1884 the house was acquired by Clarke Chapman, Engineers and converted into offices. After a fire in 1891 it was reconstructed.

Redheugh Hall was built in the late seventeenth century by the Liddell family, and held by Derwentwater's descendants. Land was lost to the railway, and the house was leased to George Hawks. Later it went into decay and was demolished in the 1930s to provide work for the unemployed.

Sir Joseph Swan (1828-1914) had his house and laboratory at Underhill, Gateshead. He invented the incadescent electric lamp, which he used in his house. Mawson & Swan's shop in Newcastle, and Mosley Street were electrically lit.

Sir William Armstrong had his country house at Cragside lighted by electricity. In 1881 Swan, Armstrong, J. T. Merz and Spence Watson formed Swan's Electric Light Company. This was the new form of lighting in time to take over from gas.

Charles Parsons lived at Park House, Gateshead for a time and carried out experiments. In 1877 he had joined Clarke Chapman, where he carried out his turbine experiments. Then all joined forces with Swan to form the Sunbeam Lamp Company to manufacture electric lamps for street lighting. In the winter of 1886 at Swan Pond on Gateshead Fell there was a sensational night display of electricity to illuminate skating.

A portable turbine driven electric generating plant, consisting of a locomotive boiler with a Parson's turbine and a direct coupled Clarke Chapman dynamo fitted on top of the boiler, the whole being fitted on wheels for portability by horse traction was used to provide the light from Swan's bulbs. We are not told if magic was provided, but in time fairgrounds would have this combination. In 1889 Parsons left Clarke Chapman to form his own company at Heaton. The ship *Turbinia* was powered by a steam turbine, and in 1897 appeared uninvited at the Royal Naval Review off Spithead, circling the giant warships at a speed of 34½ knots.

In 1889 Gateshead became a County Borough. The Town Hall was built 1868-70 to the designs of John Johnstone, architect of the demolished Newcastle Town Hall. The Clock Tower was added in 1892. In 1974 five councils were merged to form the Metropolitan Borough of Gateshead. Between 1983 and 1987 a new Civic Centre was built. The contractors were Brims & Co. who built the Northumberland County Hall at Morpeth. The Gateshead building stands three storeys high. There is a central pavilion with four similar pavilions attached to each corner, built in courtyard style and linked together. Traditional building materials have been used with pantile roofs. All the departmental headquarters were brought together to the one building. Four stained glass windows depict the theses — 'Achievement', 'Construction and Design', 'Education, Science and Culture' and 'Sport and Recreation'. The four windows are linked in design by the river which flows at the foot of each one. Gateshead has much to provide under each heading. The Sports Stadium for example, is internationally famous.

William Wailes, the famous stained glass artist, lived at Saltwell Tower amid extensive parkland. When he died in 1881, Joseph Shipley took up residence. He was a life-long collector of paintings and acquired some 2,500. Many were reproductions. By his will he offered them first to Newcastle with money for a gallery. If Newcastle refused, as they did, Gateshead was to benefit. A selection was made, and the building of the Shipley Gallery began in 1914. Saltwell Tower was acquired by the Council in 1932 to be made into a local and industrial museum. The Park with its lake had become a leisure centre, bought in 1876 from Wailes.

The Shipley Art Gallery has recently obtained 26 pieces of the finest Sowerby glass, which was manufactured in Gateshead. The items were on loan, but were presented by Mrs Marjorie Wamer, a descendant of the founder of the glassworks, so this is a most valuable acquisition. In 1807 Richard Sowerby founded what he called the New Stourbridge Glass Works, making high quality flint and coloured glass by the method of machine pressing. A wide range of objects were produced. George Sowerby and his son John increased the business with the Ellison Glass Works in East Street. By 1885 the site covered 5½ acres, and was reputed to be the biggest of its kind in the world. Men were brought from Birmingham, and there were 450 workers making 30 tons of pressed glass tableware per week. The trade mark was the family crest of the peacock.

J. C. Sowerby established a studio and brought in Venetians to make Venetian Style or Art Glass. Exhibitions of Sowerby Glass were held in other parts of the country. In 1957 the business was sold to Suntex Safety Glass, and in 1972 it was closed down. In its time it was a fine example of light, colour and beauty from Gateshead.

Metro Centre

A recent development, west of Gateshead, has been the largest out-of-town shopping centre in Europe called the Metro Centre. The indoor complex covers 115 acres with plenty of parking space. Newcastle and Gateshead together have a population of 1½ million but shoppers come from much further afield. An extended system of communications improves accessibility.

The Centre was conceived and developed by John Hall, chairman and managing director of Cameron Hall Developments. Work began in 1984 and the first shop was opened in 1986. The Centre is intended to cater for the whole family and also to provide a full range of leisure facilities. It has attracted many of the country's top names in retailing — Boots, Marks and Spencer, W. H. Smith, House of Fraser, Laura Ashley and others. Some 200 shops are now included, to be increased by another 100, making a total investment of £200 million. It will bring other developments to the area and improvements to the south bank — an example in itself of the reclamation of derelict land. The tree lined malls allow natural light to enter. There are garden areas, rest areas, play areas and restaurants. Also provided are a business park, a lake, a 150 bed hotel, a 10 screen cinema, music and pleasures for children. Much employment has been provided in the building and running of the Metro Centre.

It gets its name and connections with the rapid transit Metro Railway system, which operates on both sides of the river. The Metro bridge over the Tyne was opened in 1980. One route runs from Bankfoot (Kenton) to Gosforth, continuing by Benton, Monkseaton, and Whitley Bay to Tynemouth. The circle continues by North Shields, Wallsend, Walker, Byker to Monument and the Central Station. The route over the bridge runs to Gateshead, Heworth, Hebburn to South Shields. It is planned to make an extension to Newcastle Airport near Ponteland.

The Metro car units consist of two bodies linked by a common set of bogie wheels in the middle. These units can be coupled to make longer trains. Parts of the network within the city are underground — Haymarket, St James Monument and, in part, Manors and Byker. There are several Park and Ride car parks and some special bus link extensions. Electricity, the power for the Metro, will also be extended to the main line railway, London to Edinburgh in 1991. Coal is now used to provide power for generating electricity at some of the power stations, rather than providing direct power itself for locomotives.

Within the towns of Gateshead and Newcastle street transport had been supplied by horse drawn trams from 1860, but steam trams were not successful and from 1900 electrical traction was used. Tram cars travelling in the streets continued to run until 1951. Horse drawn brakes were used for a considerable period across the High Level Bridge, since trams were not allowed to cross till 1920.

From 1935 Trolley buses began replacing trams, but the War delayed the change. In turn trolley buses were discontinued in 1966. From 1904 an original electric train system was developed linking Newcastle and Gateshead to the coast at Tynemouth and South Shields respectively. This, with two routes north of the river, proved very effective in its time and it has been updated with the Metro system.

The newest form of transport on Tyneside has won wide acclaim and has greatly reduced traffic congestion.

Beamish

A visit to the Open Air Museum at Beamish is an ideal way of recalling past transport and travelling on a Gateshead tram. Tram No. 10 came into service in 1925 and finished in 1951 but now has a new lease of life in the museum. It advertises Newcastle Brown Ale and Walter Wilson, the smiling service grocer. Beamish, which won the Museum of the Year Award in 1986, preserves an important part of the heritage of North East England. Frank Atkinson has been the guiding genius of the scheme, and antiquities have been collected from both Northumberland and Durham by him. Work has included the rescue and re-construction of buildings — houses, and a public house to provide an image of a North East market town c. 1920. The Victorian Park there has decorative cast iron railings, a drinking fountain of 1868 and flower beds. The Victorian cast iron bandstand was transferred from Saltwell Park. In the 1970s six houses from Ravensworth Terrace, Gateshead, doomed to demolition, were transferred brick by brick to Beamish. They were fashionable Victorian middle class residences, and have been restored to illustrate the lives of a dentist, a solicitor and a family in the 1920s. Another may emerge as part of a tobacconist's shop. Also at Beamish there is a reconstructed farmhouse, a working mine and a railway powered by steam, with a replica of 'The Rocket'.

Gateshead

A man of Gateshead who deserves passing mention is James Leathart J.P. His father was a mining engineer at Alston, but James moved down the river in pursuit of his career. He was involved with the Leadworks of Foster, Blackett and Wilson in Hebburn. He bought Bracken Dene in Gateshead and produced a family of 10 children. He collected works of art, including Pre-Rapahelite pictures and china. In 1866 he was painted in his house with a view of the works through the window, discreetly veiled by a spray of leaves. This is another image of Victorian Gateshead, and this very picture was part of a very fine collection of paintings recently on display in Newcastle.

In 1990 it can be said that the country came into town. There was the exhibition at the Laing Art Gallery of the Pre-Raphaelites — Painters and Patrons in the North East. During the last century and, of course, into this industrial Tyneside was dirty, dark, dreary, polluted with coal and chemical smoke, the rivers a great sewer. But there were elements of light and colour from glass and pottery, gaslight and electricity. The industrialists were patrons of the arts, taking on what had been the role of the aristocrats and landlords. They included Sir William Armstrong, Sir Isaac Lothian Bell, Henry Bolckow and James Leathart.

A leading figure among the artists was William Bell Scott 1811 - 1890, who was appointed Master of the Government School of Design in Newcastle. He was responsible for the beautification of the cental hall at Wallington in Northumberland, the home of the Trevelyans with a series of paintings. The murals were designed to illlustrate the history of Northumberland and the Tyne played an important part — the attack of the Danes, the death of Bede, the Charlton spur and especially Iron and Coal. This panel shows the impact of industry on the river. A busy quayside and two bridges are depicted. The High Level Bridge carries a steam train and workmen are hammering the great wheels for locomotives. A girl sits on the barrel of an Armstrong gun and a steam tug with smoking funnel carries the message 'Harry Clasper for Ever'. Sailing ships and keels are shown. It was a very lively and colourful picture. You can almost hear the noise.

But the patrons generally preferred more peaceful scenes. James Leathart is painted in his colourful house at Bracken Dene, Gateshead. He was a great collector of pictures, prompted by Bell Scott, but he was discriminating. He purchased 'The Pretty Baa Lambs', a rural scene by Ford Madox Brown. Another picture 'The Hireling Shepherd' by Holman Hunt shows a young man attending to a maiden and the sheep are in the corn. The Pre-Raphaelites seemed to paint very colourful pictures of county or historical scenes in contrast to the actual environment on the Tyne. Their patrons were fond of painted glass windows and decorations in the William Morris style. William Armstrong had collections at Jesmond Dene, Cragside and Bamburgh. The Laing Gallery has a fine collection of work by local artists and craftsmen. All these shed a different light on the Tyne.

In 1990 the Gateshead Garden Festival had the idea of bringing the country into the town, and at the same time replacing the industrial scars of the past. The thronging crowds were not working, but seeking entertainment from the scenery, the music and the company of people. Steam engines have gone out of use, but little steam railways took people round the pleasure parks. A steamer cruised on the river and most of the river craft were for entertainment — rowing, sailing and surfing. There were regattas which recall the old river races and fetes. The river staiths were an industrial necessity for loading coal on ships, and they were remarkable pieces of engineering. Dunston Staiths have been preserved as a part of the riverside heritage. They were constructed from massive timbers by the North East Railway Company. There is over 1700 feet of braced timber in their construction. They were closed in 1980, but have escaped demolition and have become the equivalent of a riverside pier.

At Derwenthaugh timber piles, recovered from the river have been used to fashion a ten acre marina, which has proved very popular. It has been the venue for Water Ski-ing Championships and other kinds of water sports.

In September 1989 an unusual craft called the 'Eager Beaver' was launched at Hebburn. It was built by workers on Employment Training at Hebburn and Middlesborough and officially named 'County Durham'. It is 26 feet long and is intended to clean up the river and its banks for the benefit of sporting enthusiasts and nature lovers. It has a hydraulic scoop which deposits debris in a skip on the deck. There is a crane to deposit skips ashore and pick up heavier objects. It is supported by the four local Councils, Northumbria Water and the Quayside Development. Floating debris is both an eyesore and a danger, and the boat will help the cleaning process, all the more important for 1990s with demands for the improvement of the environment.

The Garden Festival, emulating that of Glasgow in 1988, is an example of what can be done to revive desolate areas. Gardens and parks, trees and flowers have taken over from industrial waste. Houses and pavilions have been erected where once there were coke ovens, tar works, gas works and railway sidings. The whole area was an overgrown rubbish tip and reclamation was on the grand scale. It is hoped that the pattern of recovery will be an example and that such developments will continue despite financial stringency.

Gateshead is well known in the sporting world with its Stadium, where athletes like Brendan Foster, Steve Cram and Mike McLeod, to name but a few, have performed. The Great North Run (1990) attracted more than 30,000 entries, providing a magnificent spectacle. In August 1989, at the Gateshead Stadium, the British Men's Athletic Team won the European Cup, beating the Russians and East Germans into 2nd and 3rd places respectively.

One is also reminded of Harry Clasper, who often rowed against local and national opposition from Scotswood Bridge to the High Level Bridge, with excited crowds on either bank. He designed and constructed his own boats and was truly famous in his time. A book has been written about him. On November 25th 1845 *The skiff race for £100 between Clasper of Newcastle and Pocock of London took place on the Tyne, in the presence of several thousands of spectators, Clasper, at the termination being at least a quarter of a mile in advance.*

On March 24th 1858 *A skiff race for about £100 came off this afternoon between the celebrated Harry Clasper and Matthew Taylor. Clasper went in an easy winner by 150 yards.*

On June 16th 1858 *A race with four oar skiffs took place between the families of Clasper and Taylor. There were great crowds and much excitement since the Taylors*

153

took an early lead, but the Claspers gained and won an excellent race by almost two boat lengths. The race was for £50 and the four-oared championship of the Tyne.

On July 22nd 1858 There was a great rowing mach on the Clyde between Clasper of Newcastle and Campbell, the champion of Scotland. Clasper won by 150 yards in a boat built by himself, gaining £100 and the championship.

Harry Clasper was buried in Whickham graveyard with a memorial, a canopied statue of a bearded man with his right elbow resting on a pillar and an inscription — *in this sacred spot commanding a full view of that noble river, rest the mortal remains of Henry (Harry) Clasper, the celebrated oarsman and boat builder of Derwenthaugh who died July 12 1870, aged 58.*

How well he knew the river Tyne.

Gateshead Festival has attracted more than 3 million visitors and seems to have been a great success.

Chapter Eight. EAST OF NEWCASTLE

In 1835 with the local government changes, Newcastle was empowered to take over areas such as Heaton, Jesmond and Byker, allowing more rapid expansion with increasing industrial development. The artisans had to live near the place of their labours, while the masters could live in the larger houses of Gosforth and Jesmond. The works were usually close to the river. In 1851 Shields Road was a country lane and Heaton was a village of 435 people. Byker had 7,000, but by 1911 the population of Heaton was 21,912 and Byker housed 48,709 and merged into Walker.

Heaton

Before 1297 Adam of Jesmond had built a tower 300 yards east of the Ouseburn at Heaton. Edward I stayed there, but in time it fell into ruin and the remains are at Heaton Park. From 1755 to 1841 Heaton Hall belonged to the Ridleys, who had mining interests in the area. In 1841 they sold the property, but some Heaton Hall stonework was transferred to Blagdon Hall. The church of St Gabriel at Heaton, a fine building with a tower was built 1898 - 1905 by F. W. Rich, and St. Barnabas, built by Hicks and Charleswood, is unusual in having an apse at each end.

Charles Parsons established his engineering works at Heaton which constructed turbines for his experimental ship '*Turbinia*'. Heaton became a railway junction with large engine sheds. The main Edinburgh line and the coastal lines pass through it. Newcastle United first played football at Heaton Junction, before transferring in 1885 to St James's Park, an intake from the Town Moor.

Jesmond

Jesmond has the medieval chapel of St Mary, now in ruins, which dates from the 12th century. Later part of the ruins were known as a hospital and St Mary's holy well, running with warm water, was reputed to work miracles. The Brandlings had acquired the property and dismantled the chapel before 1562. The manor house had been demolished, but Stote's Hall survived. It carried the arms of the Newcastle Merchant Adventurers over the door with the date 1607. Jesmond Parish Church was built to the designs of John Dobson 1858 - 61, impressive with a pinnacled tower. Dobson also designed the ornamental entrance of the cemetery. St George's Church, Osborne Road, was built and furnished at the expense of Charles Mitchell, Armstrong's partner. He was a painter himself and had much to do with design (1888). It is a tall building and the decoration with mosaics has been described as rather lavish or 'Art Nouveau'. Mitchell's monument is within the church, though the whole church is a monument to him. He had a house in Jesmond Dene, and Armstrong also acquired property here. He closed the Dene, planting trees and shrubs for ornament. The landscape was laid out with walks, and bridges were built, as well as the Banquetting Hall designed by Dobson. In 1880 an area called Armstrong Park was given to the city of Newcastle and in 1883 he presented the pleasure grounds of Jesmond Dene for the benefit of the people.

By 1891 the population of Jesmond had reached 8,442, but in the following years it increased rapidly to 21,367 in 1914. In 1907 the Royal Grammar School moved from Rye Hill to premises in Eskdale Terrace, Jesmond, where it is still. It has more than 400 years of history, founded in Henry VIII's reign by Thomas Horsley and housed originally at St, Nicholas. In 1600 it received a charter form Queen Elizabeth I, and took up new premises in the Virgin Mary Hospital.

Walker

Walker was once a riverside township belonging to the De Merlays, barons of Morpeth. Its name is derived from the Roman Wall hereabouts — 'Wall-Carr', meaning the marsh by the wall. Land was purchased here by the corporation to provide more space for ballast shores. The stream was filled in and the land extended. It became an important place for shipbuilding. In 1840 Coutts built a paddle steamer *Prince Albert* which had iron plates in its construction, and this was followed by *Q E D*, the first ship to carry water ballast. The designer was a certain Charles Mitchell, who was apprenticed in the firm of Wm. Simpson, Aberdeen where Coutts had also worked.

Coutts had purchased four acres of land on the Tyne at Walker to start his shipbuilding yard, which later became the Neptune Yard of John Wigham Richardson.

Charles Mitchell was born in 1799 in Aberdeen, his father a cooper and fish merchant. On leaving school he became an apprentice draughtsman with William Simpson, ironfounders. He studied chemistry at Marischal College and made a hobby of carving wooden ships as models for clients. He joined Coutts on the Tyne in 1842, but in 1844 he went to London, where he continued in marine engineering and draughtsmanship. Also he studied languages. In 1852 he was determined to set up his own shipbuilding yard at Walker next to the Iron and Alkali works. In 1854 he married Anne, daughter of William Swan, at Walker Parish Church.

Like Coutts he was determined to build iron ships, which were not yet proven. Mitchell's yard built some 450 ships between 1853 and 1882, many of which were sold abroad. Paddle steamers were sent for navigation of the river Nile. From 1857 Charles Mitchell sold paddle steamers to Russia. He knew the Russian language and undertook to train Russian staff. His brother in law,

155

Henry Swan, took charge in St Petersburg. Mitchell eventually received an Imperial medal, and in 1871 he entertained the Russian High Admiral, the Grand Duke Constantine at Jesmond Towers.

William Armstrong's firm had manufactured much field artillery and obviously guns might be fitted to warships. Armstrong approached Mitchell about the building of suitable ships to carry the guns. Andrew Noble was the gunnery expert. Eventually the new firm of Armstrong Mitchell came about and warships were built for other countries, including China and Japan. The first oil tanker was built for a German owner and cable laying vessels were also constructed. For Russia Mitchell provided ice breakers and a railway ferry.

Mitchell was benefactor to Walker, building the Mechanics Institute and Hall in 1861 and Walker Accident Hospital in 1870. His son became an artist, and Charles himself was a collector of works of art. The extension at Jesmond Towers were used for this purpose. Here he changed the landscape and built Jesmond Church, on the model of St Mark's Venice. Having been brought up in Aberdeen, he must have been impressed by seeing St Nicholas Church in Newcastle with a tower like that of Aberdeen University. Later he financed building projects in the place of his birth — a Graduation Hall and Students Union building. The tower of Marischal College was raised to a height of 220 feet, a fine memorial to Mitchell. He died on August 22nd, 1895, two days before the ceremonial opening. However, his portrait, painted by his son, Charles William, was there in time. In 1901 the artist was given the freedom of the city, an honour which would have greatly pleased his father. The Laing Gallery has a number of Charles William's paintings, the most important being 'Hypatia'. Another hangs in Blyth Public Library.

In the nineteenth century the foreshore at Wallsend was being reclaimed with river front factories and shipyards. Collieries were developed on the higher ground, the most famous being the Rising Sun, which closed in 1969. Another at Bigges Main was on an early wagonway from Gosforth to river staiths. In 1813 Blenkinsopp gave trial upon it to an early locomotive and George Stephenson had a house at Willington Quay. At West Chirton, on Middle Engine Lane, is the Stephenson Railway Museum Project. Here are housed Stephenson railway relics and locomotives.

Wallsend

Wallsend got its name from the fact that it was the eastern terminus of Hadrian's Wall with a fort and a length of Wall going down to the Tyne. At this point the river could not be forded and the steep slope would be a deterrent to attackers. In modern times the meaning of Wallsend would seem to refer to its demolition, since it almost completely disappeared under shipyards; much stone had been previously used for housing and walls. But in recent years the site of the fort has been carefully excavated, so that in some ways more is known about it than any other fort on the Wall. It was intended to develop the area for light industry, but a change of heart or mind had taken place and it has become a historical site for visitors.

The fort covers four acres with three principal gateways north of the wall. It was discovered that the area had been under cultivation before the Romans took over. The fort was built of stone and had a strong surrounding wall with towers at the corners and guarding the gates. There were ten barracks, six in the northern half and four in the south. In the centre was the headquarters with offices and assembly places. On one side was the hospital and two granaries; on the other the commandant's house. There were also workshops and on either side between the central buildings and barracks, there was space for parade and exercising. Unlike some forts on the Wall, the gateways had no partial blocking and continued open as double gateways. During a long period of occupation there were changes — barracks in the third century were changed into chalets with separate accommodation. Later still in the fourth century some timber-strip-like houses were constructed, and it has been suggested, for family occupation. The fort site has been marked out on the ground, and there is a Heritage Centre adjacent in Buddle Street, which helps with interpretation, archaeology, local history and shipbuilding, which still goes on. John Buddle, honoured in this way, was a colliery viewer.

Wallsend and Willington, in the Middle Ages, belonged to the Prior and Convent of Durham. After the Dissolution, Willington passed into lay hands, wheras Wallsend was part of the endowment of the Dean and Chapter of Durham. The old chapel of Holy Cross, consisted of nave and chancel, and its ruins still stand on the top of the steep hillside. It fell into disrepair and was said to be the haunt of witches. The new church of St Peter was built from 1807 to 1809 and enlarged in 1892. The font is that from Holy Cross. A new church was built for the west parish in 1866 with a tower to the east end and dedicated to St. Luke.

In 1800 Wallsend was a village with seven farms — Wallsend Hall, Mount Pleasant, Village Farm, Red House, The Grange and Middle Farm, White House and Carville Hall. The latter was formerly Cosyns Hall. Cosyn was a Newcastle draper, and Horsley c. 1720 noted a number of Roman stones built into his house. In the garden was an old sundial inscribed:

Time tide doth haste. Therefore, make haste We shall (die all) is implied by the dial itself.

The hall was rebuilt c. 1750 by another draper, Robert Carr, related to the Carrs of Etal and renamed Carville. In the late nineteenth century the estate was purchased by Joseph Wigham Richardson, and the hall pulled down. Mount Pleasant was purchased by Wallsend Slipway Company. Swan Hunter took over the lands of the Alkali Works and used them for their east shipyard.

At that time shipbuilding was predominant and in 1903 Swan Hunter combined with Wigham Richardson of Walker. In 1906 to the delight of all around on a public holiday they launched their vessel, the 'Mauretania' of 31,938 tons. This and a sister ship the 'Lusitania' were built for the Cunard Company and they were the pride of the Tyne. They won back the Blue Riband of the Atlantic from the Germans and held it for 22 years. In 1915 'Lusitania' was brutally sunk by a German U-Boat. The 'Ark Royal' (1981) and the 'Esso Northumbria' (1968) (253,000 tonns) were more impressive in some ways, but never more admired than 'Mauretania' powered by Parson's turbines.

157

Pevsner in his book on Northumberland buildings admired the Coal Cleaning Plant at the Rising Sun Colliery and the offices of Swan Hunter. *They are up to date the most noteworthy pieces of modern architecture in the county.*. He liked the Ship Model Gallery, the Drawing Office and 'handsome canteen'.

An incident often recorded about Wallsend is when Prince Nicholas of Russia, from 1825 known as the 'Iron Tsar', had arranged to visit Wallsend Colliery. Having put on his protective gear, he was taken to the pithead. Seeing the black hole, he was afraid and likened it to 'the mouth of hell', so the earth did not receive its distinguished visitor.

Willington

Willington Quay was the place where George Stephenson set up house after his marriage in Newburn Church (1802). In 1803 his son Robert was born here. The cottage has gone, but is remembered in the 'Stephenson Memorial Schools'. George Stephenson was self-educated, but he made sure that his son had proper schooling as well as practical training in engineering. The Stephensons moved on, but the Willington viaduct is a reminder of railways — 1,050 feet long, 76 feet high with 7 segmental arches each of 120 feet span. At Willington there was a haunted house — Willington Mill, subject to all kinds of unnatural noises and ghosts that drove residents away.

Willington had a ropery, taken over from 1900 by Hood Haggie and Clellands who established a ship repairing yard. There were other industries but Howden Pans was obviously famous for salt. There were salt pans here when the property belonged to the Prior of Durham and these continued. Salt was most important for the preservation of meat and fish. From 1702 salt was taxed, and a report on Howden Salt Pans 1725 ran —

Each pan makes one tun and a quarter of salt at 8 boilings, which lasts 3½ days...The wages of Pumpers i.e. those people who pump the salt water out of the river into the pans, is 5d per day. The Watchers i.e. those who continually have an eye to the pans and the fire stoves have 6d a day. What salt is sold here for 25s produces to the government £6 6s.

Probably on account of severe taxation the salt pans were given up after 1787.

Glass making was started in Howden in the first half of the seventeenth century — glass makers were brought in from Lorraine. One family were Tyzacks — John Tyzack, a Quaker, lived at Howden Hall. The Henzells also appear as owners of glassworks, and Joshua was manager at the time when they transferred to Lemington as the Northumberland Glass Company. The shore at Howden proved difficult for shipbuilding. The dredging of the river raised the water level and caused floods. From 1866 the level of the land was raised by ballast from ships and Howden Hall, the oldest house in the parish was demolished. A popular local song was founded on the fact that here was the place where the river was crossed at Jarrow.

> *Thors chemicals, copper, coals, clarts, coke an' stone,*
> *Iron shops, wooden tugs, salt an' saadust and' bone,*
> *Manure, an' steam-ingins, bar iron an' vitriol,*
> *Grunstans an' puddlers (aa like to te litt'ral),*

At Howdon for Jarrow, Howdon for Jarrow,
Howdon for Jarrow, maa hinnies, loup oot.
Nowadays Howden to Jarrow has another form of crossing — under the river. In 1951 a pedestrian and cycle tunnel was opened to the public, and in 1967 a much larger tunnel for motor vehicles, relieving some of the strain on the bridges, but traffic was still too crowded. Ferries still operate across the river.

North Shields

Shiels or shielings were fishermen's huts on the river bank, and in time North Shields took its name to distinguish it from the settlement at South Shields on the Bishop of Durham's side. Both groups of fishermen could be said to be in the service of the church, since there were monastic institutions at Tynemouth and Durham.

76. North Shields Fish Quay.

The focus of the settlement was the Powburn, a tributary of the Tyne. The houses had quays and some trade developed since fish was so much in demand as well as other supplies to ships. This infuriated the burgesses of Newcastle who claimed control of river trade, and in 1297 Nicholas Scot, the mayor, led an attack on North Shields and did much damage. The burgesses claimed that the prior was taking away their trade with baking and brewing to supply ships, not simply supplying the priory. The King, they claimed, was being deprived of payment. It was decided that ships were not to load or unload at Shields and merchantmen were not to be supplied there. Henry VI favoured the priory, so there were quays, bakehouses, breweries and mills at Shields, but attacks continued. Later from 1539 the Crown took over monastic properties here and the Earl of Northumberland acquired the land.

The development of coal mining and the allied salt trade also annoyed Newcastle, but salt was beyond their control. They were determined to prevent the loading of coal, and Ralph Gardner was imprisoned for refusing to close his

159

brewery (1653) which might supply ships. This provoked him to make his petition to Parliament against the demands of Newcastle.

Despite difficulties, North Shields continued to grow, the houses being concentrated near the river. They were described as crowded and unhealthy and subject to plagues. Pigs roamed freely in the streets and scavenged in the rubbish. From 1694 the streets were forbidden to pigs. About 1720 Warburton described North Shields as *a large, well built and popular seaport situated at the very confluence of the River Tyne with the sea, which there is a haven sufficient to contain a thousand ships of the largest burden.* He added *It drives a great trade in salt made of sea water and in fish, which are here cured to admiration, particularly the incomparable salmon, which they supply to most parts of Europe.*

The salt trade declined, but fishing continued to flourish, and North Shields Fish Quay is still famous in the world of fish today.

In the later part of the eighteenth and early nineteenth centuries the town extended northwards, and the port developed extensive trade with the colonies. In 1806 a Market Place was established on New Quay. A Library and Town Clock were set up in Howard Street, and in 1825 a Scientific and Mechanical Institute followed. The Duke of Northumberland was responsible for buildings on New Quay. The new town centre was called Northumberland Square, which had a fine range of buildings and a central garden area. Howard Street too has some excellent buildings including the Scotch Church (1811) by Dobson, also his Baptist Church of 1807. Dobson was architect of the Town Hall built 1844 in Saville Street.

Dockwray Square, now to be renamed Laurel Square, after Stan Laurel who lived there, overlooking the Tyne was the first urban improvement begun in 1763 by Thomas Dockwray, vicar of Stamfordham. Two centuries later it has gone and the area has been redeveloped. Notable buildings hereabouts are the Old High Light built in 1727 and, at a lower level, the New High Light of 1808, both prominent features overlooking the river and serving the port by guiding ships to harbour.

In 1832 Tynemouth, including North Shields, Preston and Chirton, became a Parliamentary Borough, and in 1836 the centre of a Poor Law Union. Later from 1849 it became a municipal Borough. In 1833 Custom House Officers of North Shields were empowered to clear without reference to Newcastle, costwise vessels loading below Hebburn Point, and in 1848 Shields became an independent customs port with a custom house at Shields. The boundary was from Whitehill Point to Jarrow Quay. In 1865 North and South Shields became separate ports, and until 1897 Blyth was included in the port of North Shields.

From 1850 the Tyne Improvement Commission took over the care of the river from Newcastle Corporation, and Tynemouth provided three of fourteen members. From 1854 the Commissioners began the task of constructing piers at the entrance of the river to improve navigation. It turned out to be a lengthy task. Dredging is a ceaseless operation. Tynemouth bar was removed and sands and shoals along the river. In 1857 the Northumberland Dock was opened, and in 1884 the Prince of Wales opened what was called the Albert Edward Dock.

In 1877 William Purdy of North Shields, owner of steam tugs that hauled sailing trawlers out to sea, had the idea of using them as steam trawlers. By 1909, 76 steam trawlers were based at North Shields and 20,000 tons of herrings were landed annually. It was accompanied by a great movement of fish workers, since a lot of foreign vessels came in. There were factories for curing and processing fish. In Northumberland Square from 1814 was set up a local 'deity', the figure of Dolly, a fishwife. Pieces of wood from her were taken as good luck tokens, so that in time she was much disfigured. She has been restored five times to date.

The local church, Christ Church, was originally built up by Robert Trollop (1658-68). It was largely rebuilt in 1792; the west tower was built in 1786. The neighbouring public house is called the Old Hundredth, and another famous hostelry is the Northumberland Arms. The fourth Duke was responsible for building the Sailor's Home, providing accommodation for 80 visiting sailors. A modern description runs — *The whole quayside area is worth a visit — the local authority has prepared a sound development plan and swept away many of the old derelict premises replacing them with hygienic new fish processing units, built on the site of Clifford's Fort.* There is a lot of activity in the town and along the riverside. A local history Centre and the Library provide visitors with information.

Another adjacent area was Chirton. The hall there was knocked down in 1811 when Burdon Main Colliery was opened, and Mr Lawson, the proprietor, moved to Cramlington Hall. For a time Admiral Collingwood held land he inherited at Chirton, but on his death (1810), it passed to another branch of the family.

For long a landmark in the neighbourhood was Billy (formerly Billings) Mill The windmill existed as early as 1320 and was rebuilt for the Earl of Northumberland in the years 1597-9. In 1659 it was in danger when Ralph Gardner quarried all round it. In 1760 it was burnt down and rebuilt only to become a ruin in modern times. It is a great pity there is no working windmill locally. In West Chirton, industrial development began in 1799 with the winning of Percy Main Colliery. A modern village was built for the miners and the name took over. The river front was used for ballast and docks. It was here at the junction with the Coble Burn that the Albert Edward Dock, 1884, was constructed.

North Shields merges into Tynemouth, appropriately since at one time most of the land belonged to Tynemouth Priory, where the church was used till the building of Christ Church, and where the dead were buried for many years after. In 1658 a petition at the Morpeth quarter sessions ran *there is the great want of a church there, whereby not only the parishioners, but many others, both masters of shipps, straingers and other travellers and passengers, resorting thither cannot have any publique and convenient place for the service and worship of God, the former church being made use of for the garrison of Tynemouth Castle, soe that some thousands of people ar left destitute of the word and means of salvation, to the great dishonour of God and encouragement of many loose and ignorant people prophaneing of the sabboth and liveing in lewd life and conversation.*

For many a time a malting kiln at Chirton, belonging to Ralph Gardner, was used, but the new church was consecrated in 1668 by the Bishop of Durham, and Dr Dockwray held the first service there. Large pews were provided for the

161

Duke, Sir Ralph Delaval and officers of Tynemouth Castle. In 1792 with a growing population it had to be rebuilt. It did not take the name of either St. Mary or St Oswin that were used at Tynemouth Priory.

Tynemouth

Tynemouth from its name is situated where the river reaches and argues with the sea. There is a rocky headland, some seventy feet above the sea, almost detached by a deep ditch and on the platform stand the remains of a castle, a priory (which was also the parish church) and a watch-house. It is not usual for all these to be combined in one place. The Romans would know the landscape feature, looking across to their fort at South Shields and, if there was no fort here, there may well have been some kind of lighthouse.

81. View of Tynemouth.

Today it is possible to stand here and imagine the ships that have passed. Roman transport ships came to South Shields with provisions for the Wall and to provide food for warriors attempting the conquest of Caledonia (Scotland). Anglo Saxons came here as raiders, then settlers and they were used to sea travel, so that monks and nuns could exchange visits by ship. Cargoes of timber and other products were conveyed by sea. In medieval times there were merchant vessels and warships built locally of timber to serve the King in the Scottish and Foreign Wars. At the time of the Spanish Armada (1588) Tynemouth was a fortress and the Spanish battery overlooked the mouth of the river. Troops were here during the Civil War, the Jacobite Rebellions and the Napoleonic Wars. Military and religious claims to the site were often in conflict. The great sailing ships have passed, the fishing boats, the colliers, the tugs, the tankers, bulk carriers and passenger liners. Many of each kind were built on the River Tyne.

The Anglo Saxons had a church here, but only fragments of crosses remain. In 792 came the first attack of the Danes, who did great damage and here at

162

Jarrow, though they suffered repulse in a battle at Jarrow Slake. In 800 they came again and the church seemed to suffer eclipse, but was restored later. In 1065 a priest here, named Edmund, dreamed that King Oswin was killed and buried here. He and others dug under the floor of the church and found a coffin with bones that they considered were those of the saint. In 1070 during the Northern Rebellion the Normans attacked the abbey to get provisions. Afterwards Earl Waltheof granted Tynemouth to the monks of Jarrow. These monks were later recalled to Durham, and Robert de Mowbray the new Earl, granted Tynemouth to the Abbey of St Albans in 1085. This was for long a matter of dispute between Durham and St Albans. In 1093 Malcolm Canmore, King of Scotland, killed at Alnwick, was buried here. The body later returned to Dunfermline was said not to be his.

Robert de Mowbray had a castle here at Tynemouth, which was taken by the King in 1095 during Mowbray's rebellion. Mowbray, defeated became a monk of St. Albans. Durham again claimed Tynemouth.

At this time a new Norman church was built at Tynemouth Priory and the remains of St. Oswin were brought back from Jarrow. The church consisted of a nave with aisles, transepts with a tower between and a chancel with apses. Durham still laid claim to Tynemouth, and it was not till 1174 that the matter was resolved in favour of St Albans. The southern monastery seems to have used Tynemouth as a kind of 'Siberian' place of exile for refactory (disobedient) monks. We have a rather pitiful letter from one exile to his friends that must have persuaded them to behave better

Our house is confined to the top of a high rock and is surrounded by the sea on every side. Here is the approach to the monastery through a gate cut out of the rock, so narrow that a cart can hardly pass through. Day and night the waves break and roar and undermine the cliff. Thick sea frets roll in, wrapping everything in gloom. Dim eyes, hoarse voice, sore throats are a consequence. Spring and summer never come here. The north wind is always blowing and it brings with it cold and snow, or storms in which the wind tosses the salt sea-foams in masses over our buildings and rains it down within the castle. Shipwrecks are frequent. It is a great pity to see the numbed crew whom no power on earth can save, whose vessel, mast swaying and timbers parted, dashes upon rock or reef. No ring dove or nightingale is here, only grey birds which nest in the rocks and greedily prey upon the drowned, and whose screaming cry is a token of coming storm. The people who live by the seashore feed upon black malodorous seaweed called 'slank', which they gather on the rocks. Men, women and children are as dark as Africans or swarthiest Jews. In the spring the sea air blights the stunted fruit trees, so that you will find yourselves lucky to find a wizened apple, though it will set your teeth on edge should you try to eat it. See to it, dear brothers, that you do not come to so comfortless a place. But the church is of wonderous beauty. Within it lies the body of the blessed martyr Oswin in a silver shrine, magnificently embellished with gold and jewels. He protects the murderers, thieves and seditious persons who fly to him and commutes their punishment to exile. He heals those whom no physician can cure. The martyr's protection and the church's beauty furnish us with a bond of unity. We are well off for food, thanks to the abundant supply of fish, of which we never tire.

The account emphasises that the priory could be a sanctuary for malefactors, if they escaped arrest, and could not be taken within the church or its limits. They had to abjure their homeland when they got out, and if they returned were liable to the full severity of the law. The Monks's Stone was probably a marker for the limit of the sanctuary and it was inscribed with the words — *O horrid deed, to kill a man for a pigges hede.* The story was that a monk from Tynemouth, passing Lord Delaval's hall at Seaton Delaval saw a pig's head, which he purloined. When he discovered this, Delaval pursued the monk, caught him and handled him so severely that he died a year later. Delaval had to do penance and give lands to the priory for compensation.

William Turner, whose *Herbal* has been reprinted, wrote that the poorer classes of Northumberland did eat 'slauk' (slank), together with leeks and onions.

They put in a pott and snore it, as they call it, and then it loketh black and then they would put oyniones to it and eat it. But before it is sodden it is wonderful grene.

He said it was like lettuce and *it groweth in the sea abvout shelles and stones also. It coloth and dryeth.*

He also described the birds nesting at Tynemouth on the cliffs, and these seem to have been cormorants. Turner, who once lived in Morpeth, died in 1568.

In the thirteenth century the chancel of the monastic church was rebuilt and almost doubled in length — four bays were added to five; and the nave was extended. The present remains indicate that it must have been an imposing building with tall arches and long lancet windows. It was wider than the older building and higher, so that the old building could still be used inside while the new one was being built. The nave was for use as a parish church and so the monks needed more space for their own services and processions. The nave was closed from the chancel by a stone screen beneath the west wall of the central tower. The length of the church was now 261 feet, and in the mid-fifteenth century it was extended by the building of the little chapel and the east end, called the Percy Chapel. It has elaborate cross ribs for the vaulting with ornamental bosses and is attractively decorated.

The church was central to an enclosure of 12 acres. On the south side were the monastic buildings around the cloister — the dormitory to the east, the kitchen and refectory on the south. Gardens extended eastwards from the church and the farm buildings were to the north. There were barns, byres and stables. Places for pigs and poultry, bakehouse and brewery were there also. The monks were entitled to a daily ration of ale, which was the usual drink. There were fish ponds to keep the fish for monks. Meat was for those in the Infirmary and for visitors of all kinds, including royalty. The monastery was completely self-sufficient, but there were shortages during the Scottish Wars.

It was this threat that led to the building up of defences. In 1297 King Edward I, after a visit, gave a licence to fortify the priory and make it a castle. A strong gatehouse was built, and the priory was able to hold out against attacks by Gilbert de Middleton (1317).

Supplies in time of shortage were provided by the King. Prior Thomas de la

164

Mare did some rebuilding, but after the Black Death in 1348, he became Abbot of St. Albans (1350 - 1390). There was still trouble at Tynemouth from the wars, and the gatehouse with Barbican had to be rebuilt. The Prior's Haven provided a convenient harbour, but the days of the monasteries were numbered. In 1536 Henry VIII's agents visited Tynemouth which had a prior and fifteen monks, seven of whom were severely criticised as immoral. When they surrendered in 1539 they were well treated and pensioned. The King took over the property, moveables were sold and valuables were carted away. Henry VIII also appropriated all the lands of the priory and the castle was needed for local defence. In 1544 Tynemouth was the base for an English fleet to invade Scotland, and Italian experts made plans for improving the fortifications. There were outworks in front of the gatehouse, and a battery on the other side of Prior's Haven, called the Spanish Battery because for a time it was manned by Spaniards (mercenaries). Sir Thomas Hilton was in charge of the priory and after his death, Sir Henry Percy was made captain (1559). He found it a difficult task since Queen Elizabeth wanted to cut the cost of keeping fifty soldiers there.

Percy was fined for not maintaining the place properly and deprived of office. He died in prison 1585 and Robert Carey took over. The castle was put into a better state of repair in the year of the Armada and was described thus —

Tynemouth glories in a splendidly fortified castle. In 1591 the new Earl of Northumberland was restored to the captaincy of Tynemouth. At the end of the century the castle was going into decay and there only twenty able men there. In 1605 the Earl of Northumberland was unwittingly involved in the Gunpowder Plot through his agent and relative, Thomas Percy. The Earl was imprisoned for many years in the Tower and fined £30,000. Tynemouth was granted to the Earl of Dunbar, a Scottish favourite of James I, who considered defence unnecessary with the union of the Crowns. But Sir William Selby as captain did his best for a time to maintain the place, which had been robbed in the interval. His successor Sir John Fenwick (1616) found it so ruinous as hardly fit to lodge in. In spite of various schemes put forward little was done but one proposal to replace it with a block house was not carried out.

With the approach of the Bishop's War in 1640 against the Scots, it was decided to concentrate on Newcastle. Leslie's men, when they took over Tynemouth, were able to put a stranglehold on the coal trade. The King had to make peace, but Civil War followed and the Earl of Newcastle made some attempt to restore the defences of Tynemouth and guns were installed. But after the Royalist defeat at Marston Moor 1644 and the capture of Newcastle, Tynemouth, hit by plague, surrendered to the Scots. Later in dispute with Parliament (1646) the Scots turned to support Charles I, who came to Tynemouth and dined in the castle. When negotiations failed, the King planned to escape on a Dutch ship, but in vain. During the second Civil War (1648) Parliament restored the defences of Tynemouth and Newcastle. Colonel Lilburn, at Tynemouth Castle declared for the King, but he was defeated and put to death. Colonel Fenwick took charge of the troops, but was afterwards sent to Berwick as Governor. Tynemouth had to be maintained and in 1660 when Charles II became King, Colonel Villiers became captain of Tynemouth

Castle. In 1664 it *is well fortified, hath very good guns and guard of soldiers and a pretty fair church gone much to decay.* It had a bowling green and convenient houses. There was a watch-tower or beacon where every night a fire burned to guide ships to the port.

Villiers built himself a new house near the lighthouse and this remained till 1902. He seems to have used stone from other buildings, and further changes affected the buildings of the monastery which were converted to military use. This went on for many years, but under English Heritage, the monastic and military history of the site is exposed to public view. The gun sites can be inspected to see how they worked and cannons of various periods range across the walls. About the ruined church is a collection of interesting grave stones blackened by smoke and eroded by the winds. A specially interesting monument is to Corporal Rollo, who held the lantern at the burial of Sir John Moore on Spanish soil after the Battle of Corunna (1809).

In 1775 the old lighthouse tower was taken down and rebuilt. In 1802 an oil lamp was installed and when it was demolished in 1898 two hundred carved stones from the priory ruins were found built into the structure. With lights on each of the piers at the harbour mouth and with light-houses at St. Mary's Island to the north and Souter Point to the south, it was no longer necessary.

The river mouth has been the scene of many shipping disasters, especially before the piers were built. A dangerous reef called the Black Middens was often responsible. On 24th November 1864 a passenger ship *Stanley*, bound from Aberdeen to London, went on the rocks and twenty six lives were lost, despite the desperate efforts of coastguards and others. This and other wrecks prompted the formation of the Tynemouth Life Brigade in 1869. Their building stands beneath Collingwood's monument. It is complementary to the Lifeboat Service, and has helped to rescue the crew of many vessels since. The Watch House and Museum houses equipment that has been used. There are various mementoes and ornamental figureheads of ships that floundered near. It is an attractive place to visit with views along and across the river and out to sea. It is specially welcome on a wild and windy day — ships can be seen coming and departing.

80. Tynemouth Piers.

Tynemouth itself is a pleasant seaside resort with some eighteenth century houses along Front Street. The writer Harriet Martineau stayed in No. 57 from 1840 - 1845, and was visited by a number of eminent men and women. *Over the ridge I survey the harbour and all its traffic, the view extending from the lighthouses far to the right to a horizon of the sea to the left.* Tynemouth has continued to attract holiday visitors with its extensive sands and seaside amusements; the coast continuing to Cullercoats and Whitley Bay.

We now cross over the to the south bank of the Tyne.

Chapter Nine. SOUTH OF TYNE

Felling

Felling merges with Gateshead and seems to consist of rows of Victorian terrace houses climbing the hillside. Two imposing Victorian buildings are the Anglican Christ Church by Austin & Johnson (1866) and the Catholic St. Patrick's (1893) by Charles Walker.

Felling is famous for its Male Voice Choir, and is remembered for the terrible mining disaster of 1812, when 92 men and boys were killed in an explosion down the pit, when fire damp ignited. The Revd. John Hodgson of Jarrow and Heworth preached on this and helped to promote a movement leading to the invention of the Miner's Safety Lamp by Sir Humphrey Davy and George Stephenson. Hodgson designed his own church at Heworth, built in 1822, and an obelisk was erected in the churchyard to those killed in the colliery disaster. A different memorial is that of the Haddon children, lying under a stone four poster with pillows and bedspread, indicating terrible mortality among the young. Heworth Hall, now the Conservative Club, is a handsome house of about 1700 with five bays.

Below Heworth and Felling is Bill Quay, where the Tyne takes a turn northwards in its winding course. Here an unusual development has taken place in a derelict area. Gateshead M.B.C. has established the Bill Quay Community Farm as a recreational and educational centre. The small farm has been restored as a working entity to recreate the old farming practices. The grassland is sown with old fashioned grasses and the animals are rare breeds which have been in danger of dying out. It is reached from Pelaw, near the Co-operative Factory, and designed to encourage people, particularly children, to explore past environments.

A century ago this was a popular rhyme —

Baith side of the Tyne, aw remember
Were covered in bonny green fields,
But now there is nought but big furnaces
Down frae Newcastle to Shields.

And what wi' their sulphur and brimstone,
Their vapour, their smoke and their steam,
The grass is all gaen, and the farmers
Can nowther get butter nor cream.

The land became pitted with collieries. There were spoil heaps and way leaves — waggonways, like the Pelaw waggonway, to the staiths. Acid gases and deposits came from the alkali and paint works, not dispersed even by Clapham's 263 foot chimney at Friar's Goose. The salmon fisheries here did not survive pollution and the pastures were poisoned, so that a lot of the wild life died away. From 1953 a two million ton spoil heap was being removed from along the Felling/Bill Quay riverside to form a riverside park which was opened in 1966, and another 'no man's land', an unsightly mess, was transformed into the Community Farm with the Riverside Walk Way. Grass, flowers and butterflies have returned, friendly farm animals can be seen and old implements inspected. An excellent booklet entitled *Bill Quay, a Pictorial Essay* can be obtained which explains the farm and neighbourhood history.

Augustus Hare, travel writer, visited the area in 1876 and wrote about Jarrow that the Rector Edward Liddell and his wife *are amidst a teeming population of blackened, foul mouthed, drunken roughs, living in miserable rows of dismal houses, in a country where every vestige of vegetation is killed by noxious chemical vapours, on the edge of a slimy marsh, with a distance of inky sky & furnaces vomiting forth volumes of blackest smoke. All nature seems parched & writhing under the pollution.*

He could, however, have found pleasanter places like Monkton, which still retains some aspects of a village. The Hall, built in 1763, consisted of five bays with two storeys in pleasant grounds. Other fine houses of the same period are Monkton Farmhouse and Bede House, Grange Farmhouse and the Grange. The Church of the Venerable Bede was erected in 1881. At Monkton is Bede's Well, the use of which goes far back in time on the route of pilgrims, who tasted the waters and hoped for cures from the Saint. It has recently been restored with stone from Springwell quarry, providing a centre of interest for visitors. The Monkton Coke Works have been closed (1990).

Hebburn

Here the Church of St. John 1886 - 87 was converted from the stables of Hebburn Hall, which belonged to the coal-owning Ellison family. A seventeenth century house was rebuilt by William Newton 1790 - 92, and John Dobson made alterations in 1819 for Cuthbert Ellison. The impressive St. Andrew's Presbyterian Church here was built for the shipbuilder Andrew Leslie by Johnson in 1872. There was much shipbuilding hereabouts and industry, but attractive riverside walks have been devised and a maritime centre is being developed — Hebburn Village Ship and Shipbuilding Exhibition Centre at the famous Hawthorn Leslie Yard. A wartime destroyer *HMS Cavalier* has been acquired as a tourist attractive. Built on the Isle of Wight by J. Samuel White & Co. the 2,106 ton destroyer came to South Tyneside from Brighton Marina.

At Hebburn, Palmers had a shipyard and at present Reyrolles manufacture electrical switch gear here. At neighbouring Jarrow, Palmers established a shipyard in 1852. In time it extended to 100 acres and covered three quarters of a mile of river frontage. By 1933 it could be described as the 'place that launched a thousand ships', and then it was closed; a complete disaster for the town. In 1852 an iron screw collier named *John Bowes* was launched here. Weighing 485 tons she was the first successful steam collier and model for others. In 1906 *John Bowes* was renamed *Transit* and continued in service 'till 1933, when the vessel went down with all hands in a Bay of Biscay storm in the very year that Palmers closed.

When Palmers shipyard began, Jarrow was a small colliery village, but when Sir Charles Mark Palmer retired in 1900 it was an industrial town of some 40,000 inhabitants. Palmer concentrated his resources so that he had everything, including coal and iron supplies, under his control. Henry Ford is said to have taken the idea of production-line engineering from Palmers. In 1911 the firm leased Stephenson's shipyard at Hebburn, so the shipyards covered 40 acres. During the War 1914 - 1918, there was great prosperity in shipbuilding, but after the War came collapse in heavy industry, shipbuilding and mining. Nobody seems to have thought about it in advance and in areas committed to one industry, there was massive unemployment. Palmers at Jarrow was closed down but the Hebburn yard which had been taken over by Armstrong Vickers in 1928 survived.

Jarrow

Jarrow was described as *The town that was murdered* the title of a book by Ellen Wilkinson M.P. The misery that ensued provoked the Hunger March of 1936, which won widespread sympathy. Jarrow has recovered, but something of the old feeling remains. Life in the area has been dramatically depicted in the novels of Catherine Cookson and especially in her autobiography entitled *Our Kate*. In fact the whole of the Tyne area from Jarrow to South Shields has been called 'Catherine Cookson Country', and a Cookson Trail provided for visitors.

In time past 'the Light of the North' was the life and works of the Venerable Bede, who lived most of his life and died in the monastery of Jarrow, which overlooked Jarrow Slake. The monastery was founded in 681 by Benedict Biscop with a grant of land from King Egfrith, and it was linked with a twin monastery at Monkwearmouth. Benedict Biscop had travelled widely, several times to Rome. He was a collector of manuscripts and wished to bring culture to the North. Monasteries were centres of learning as well as places of devotion. He wanted his church to be admired and brought in craftsmen from the continent to help in the work of construction and glass making. It was dedicated to St. Paul. The dedicatory inscription stone is the oldest surviving one in the country. It records in Latin that the basilica of St. Paul was dedicated in the 15th year of King Egfrith's reign and the 4th of Ceolfrid the abbot. It is interesting to notice how dates were recorded until Bede provided our Christian chronology. He wrote a *History of the English Church and People* and the date that mattered was the birth of Christ. So we get our Anno Domini — the year of Our Lord, and this form of dating continues to our own time.

The church was built in Roman style from Roman stone, probably brought by boat from the fort at South Shields. There was a number of monastic buildings, and excavations have shown that there were two churches — the second, dedicated to St. Mary, was to the east of St. Paul's and there was a cemetery here before the churches.

Below the churches on the land sloping to the river were two buildings — a stone refectory measuring 96 by 26 feet and the Monk's Hall measuring 60 by 26 feet. Both had internal divisions. In the refectory was a stone shaft, probably the base of a reading deck, from which one monk would read while the others

169

dined. Near to the river were terraced gardens and workshops. Both glasswork and metal work were done on the site, and also the tanning of skins. Since illuminated manuscripts were produced here, so were materials for writing upon. Manuscripts were exported to the continent, and delays of work were caused by cold weather. So Jarrow was a place of scholars and Bede was writing, or in the end dictating, until the day of this death in 735, on Ascension Day.

In the *Anglo Saxon Chronicle* for 794 we read *And Northumbria was ravaged by the Heathen & Ecgfrith's monastery at Donemup (Jarrow) looted; and there one of their leaders was slain & some of their ships besides were shattered by storms: and many of them were drowned there and some came ashore alive & were at once slain at the river mouth.* The river here coming into the Tyne was called the Don, hence the old name for Jarrow. It was at this time that the church was severely damaged, the glass of the windows was smashed and treasures were taken away.

Later in Norman times the monastery and churches were restored. A tower was built up between the two churches and there was some rebuilding of these and the monastic buildings. At the present time it is the medieval remains of the monastic buildings that still stand. It had become a cell of Durham. Prior Aldwin (1074 - 83) probably built the central tower above the link building between the two churches.

In the eighteenth century St. Paul's, the nave, had to be rebuilt, but St. Mary's, the chancel, survived in its old form showing pre-Conquest work. The church, now a single entity, which survived the dissolution, is well worth detailed inspection to discover the various periods of building. The nave was again restored by Sir Gilbert Scott in 1866.

Much enlightenment may be obtained by a visit to the Bede Monastery Museum at Jarrow Hall across the green from the church. It gives a history of the monastery and displays Saxon sculptures that have been recovered by excavation. There are pottery and other relics. Some of the Jarrow manuscripts are on display, showing the skill and beauty of the work. Tools and building materials have been recovered, but most important is the glass. As stated, Benedict Biscop brought over glass makers from the continent, and the windows of Jarrow had coloured glass. The colour came from metal oxides. The glass was blown, flattened and cut into small sections, to be fitted together in a pattern. Small windows have been recreated by experts from the broken glass recovered from the monastic site.

In the musuem, medieval stone carving is on display and the layout of the medieval monastery is explained. There are other exhibitions at Jarrow Hall including one on William Jobling, who in 1832 was sentenced to be hanged and gibbetted for a murder he did not commit. The Alfred Pit had opened in 1803 and in 1832 there was a prolonged strike of the miners. On 11th June, 1832, William Jobling and Ralph Armstrong had been drinking and met Mr Nicholas Fairless, a magistrate riding near the toll gate. Jobling asked him for money, and when he refused Armstrong pulled him from his horse and so severely beat him that he died ten days later, but maintained that Jobling had not assault him. Armstrong escaped arrest, but Jobling was arrested and death sentence carried out. His body was coated with pitch and hung on a gibbet at Jarrow Slake under military guard for three weeks. After this time it disappeared and was probably buried by friends.

The Slake is a large tidal mudflat and noted as a bird sanctuary. A large part of it was used as timber seasoning ponds. The timbers were held by upright wooden posts, so that they rose and fell with the tide but could not float away. Catherine Cookson was nearly drowned by falling from them, and in one of her books, *Fifteen Streets*, the Slake took two victims. Much of it has now been reclaimed.

In 1866 the church of Christ Church with its tall broach spire was built. Sir Charles Mark Palmer provided a Memorial Hospital for Jarrow, and a statue of him was erected in the grounds in 1903. On the pedestal are bronze plaques of this two most famous ships *SS John Bowes* and *HMS Resolution*.

In 1959 a new shopping precinct was built at Jarrow and a Community Centre (1975-8). Another development by the Northumbrian Water Authority was the Preliminary Treatment Works Plant, which was carefully landscaped and allows access to the river. A further such plant is across the Tyne at Howden. Boldon Flats is a ten acre wetland Nature Reserve for wildfowl.

Boldon

Boldon deserved attention, in the first place, because it gives the name to the Boldon Book. The North East was not included in Domesday Book (1086), but in 1183 Bishop Pudsey of Durham compiled his own 'Buke' of lands of the Bishopric in Durham and Northumberland — Bedlingtonshire, Norham and Islandshire. From this survey we obtain valuable information.

East Boldon has a long street with some fine eighteenth century houses, including Boldon House and Boldon Lodge. Situated on a low hill it has commanding views across some featureless land towards the Tyne. Its church is a modern brick building 1922 - 1933.

West Boldon hill is crowned by an impressive church of St. Nicholas, which has a very fine thirteenth century broach spire. It has an attractively furnished interior with effigies of two medieval priests. Terraces and green fields divide it from industrial Tyneside, which is viewed from the churchyard. West Boldon Hall is the manor house built in 1709 by William Fawcett. Scots House, dated 1798, is a grander building with earlier eighteenth century wings and stables, entered by a Victorian Tudor gatehouse.

Boldon Mill, a three storey tower of 1834, has recently been restored with sails, and once again is a reminder of the importance of windpower for both mills and ships — natural power as opposed to coal. Boldon Colliery is described by Pevsner as 'a classic example of a Durham mining settlement', many of which are disappearing.

Continuing along the higher ground eastwards, one approaches Cleadon. This is another attractive area and Cleadon Tower dates from 1550, but there has been much change to the building since that time. Cleadon House is a good eighteenth century brick building, and Cleadon Windmill, an early nineteenth century tower mill, is a landmark for many miles around and looks over stone cottages, farmhouses and fields. Another landmark in Cleadon Park is the Pumping Station (1860 - 2) with a campanile chimney.

Whitburn

Whitburn is an attractive village near the coast; it owes its appearance to the Williamson family, local landowners here from the eighteenth to the twentieth century, who provided Members of Parliament. Their former house, Whitburn Hall, large with extensive gardens, was burnt down in 1978 and later demolished. Red Cottage and Whitburn House are rather extravagant Victorian mansions. The church dedicated to St. Andrew has a fourteenth century west tower, but the building was much restored in 1867. It contains a rather amusing recumbent effigy of Michael Mathew of Cleadon (1689) wearing a periwig. There is a windmill as a landmark, a three-storey tower, rebuilt c.1790 after being blown over.

The White Horse on Cleadon Hills is said to relate to Sir Hedworth Williamson, of Whitburn, who rode regularly with his wife along the beach. On one occasion she was riding along near Marsden Rock and disappeared together with her horse. They were never found, and her heart-broken husband gave his horses to his ostler Wareham, who as a memorial to this master and the lost wife, etched the 'white horse' on the hills.

Lewis Carroll, properly Charles Dodgson (1832 - 1898) author of *Alice in Wonderland* and other children's books, often stayed during the summer holidays at Whitburn. Among other writings the nonsense rhyme, the Walrus and the Carpenter, was written while he was here, inspired by what he saw. He probably saw a melancholy man with a walrus moustache and a bent man, gossiping sadly about the weather or lack of fish. In the poem —

The Walrus and the Carpenter were walking on the strand,
They wept like anything, they wept like anything
To see such quantities of sand.

If seven maids with seven mops swept it for half a year,
Do you suppose, the Walrus said, that they would get it clear?
I doubt it, said the Carpenter, and shed a bitter tear.

It is amusing, but is it nonsense? Mining waste is being deposited off the Durham coast and it returns to the sands. Also there is the perennial fear that some great oil slick may appear. Pollution is a great threat to the sea. Power station ash and industrial waste are still being dumped in the sea.

North of Whitburn on Lizard Point, Souter lighthouse was built in 1871 because of a number of wrecks on this dangerous coast. It is not now used and has been taken over by the National Trust, anxious to acquire and preserve as much of the coast as possible. Four miles of it from there to Sandhaven of South Shields, is a particularly attractive and varied stretch of coastline.

Marsden Bay has special geological interest and has the free standing Marsden Rock, which was once connected with the mainland. The 'stack' is the famous haunt of kittiwakes, fulmars and cormorants, ever vocal even when resting. Many migratory birds call here. Standing 100 feet high, it is engaged in an everlasting struggle with the sea, and is gradually being eroded.

Marsden Grotto was built in 1782 by a character called Jack the Blaster, a miner, who had no home for his family, so he started living in caves. These were extended and he began supplying visitors with drinks. Later Peter Allan, a gamekeeper of the Marquess of Londonderry, took over and made it into a fifteen roomed house. He also had a tavern cave, said to be used by smugglers. In 1849 he died, and the rock hewn tavern continues as a popular hostelry. It is said to be haunted by the ghost of John the Jibber, who would have betrayed his comrades to the excise men, but they suspected him and he was hoisted into a lift shaft and left to die. Frenchman's Bay takes its name from a French ship wrecked there and Trow Rocks are limestone cliffs, quarried by the Romans, and in the nineteenth century used to provide stone for building the piers on both sides of the Tyne. Hereabouts there are attractive sands and bathing, weather permitting.

Sailing and bathing can both be dangerous and rescue efforts have to be made. In 1866 the South Shields Volunteer Life Brigade was formed to assist the coastguards and lifeboatmen in times of emergency. Breeches buoy equipment could be used in some cases for persons stranded on the cliffs. The Watch House was completed in 1986 — 120 years after the organisation was formed.

South Shields

South Shields, situated at the mouth of the Tyne, overlooks the river from the south, as does Tynemouth from the north. Both places would be known to pre-Roman people. When it first appears in history South Shields has the name of the Roman fort here — Arbeia, possibly meaning 'the place where the Arabs lived'.

Here were stationed for maritime purposes a group of Tigris lightermen, who served as pilots and organised the river traffic — smaller boats supplying or unloading the larger ships. It is interesting to notice that South Shields still is the place for pilots on the Tyne. Arbeia was established as a base for the Roman conquest of North Britain, and for the extended campaign in Caledonia (Scotland).

In recent years the site of the fort has been the scene for extensive excavations. It was partly built over, but the remaining buildings have been removed so that the whole area could be investigated. It is one of the most exciting places on the Roman Wall, though strictly speaking it is not part of it. If you have visited or excavated on the other fort sites, you get used to thinking that all face south to the Tyne, but South Shields has the river to the north. The other factor that is difficult to realise — South Shields is about as far north as Gosforth on account of the northward turning of the Tyne. South Shields is about four miles from where the Wall ended, and the date of the first fort is hard to establish. The earliest constructions were of timber. Early pottery suggests that they may have been occupied as early as Agricola's campaigns in North Britain 78-84 A.D. The second century fort was built in the usual Roman pattern, but in the third century there was a great change when it was converted into a supply base.

This was done in two stages. The northern part and part of the centre were converted into granaries. The normal fort has two granaries, but here the number was much increased. Also the size of the fort was extended by removing the south wall of the fort, which was enlarged from 4.1 acres to 5.2. A wall was constructed to separate the accommodation of the troops from the area for grain storage. The headquarters building in the centre was converted into granaries and another H. Q. was built facing the other way (southwards), and not so large. Altogether there were now twenty three granaries, which could hold some 3,200 tonnes of grain, enough to feed an army of 50,000 men for more than two months. Two granaries provided for a fort housing 500 men. Later many of the granaries were converted to other uses. Excavations have shown that the nature of the barracks was changed. The old form was a rectangular building with eight or ten blocks. This was converted into a system of five double rooms.

Excavations also showed that in the final phase of the fort there had been a fire causing destruction. Usually this attributed to the attacks of the barbarians, but this may well have been accidental. For the archaeologists it provided carbonised grain and the bones of many small animals such as mice that were helping themselves to Roman rations. In the southern section of the fort, ten barrack blocks were re-established in the new style. In addition a large court-yard house had been constructed, and it is thought that this might have been the residence of the commander of Tigris bargemen.

Occupation of the site continued beyond the Roman period, and Leland called Caer Urffa, which was the birthplace of Oswin, King of Deira. The kingdom north of the river was called Bernicia, and the two combined to form 'Northumbria'.

For more than a century, the area of the Roman fort has been under the care of the local authority. Excavations from 1875 showed buildings of two different types of stone, of two different periods and the foundations were preserved by putting two different types of concrete on them for preservation. In 1949 Professor Ian Richmond carried out further excavations, and in 1953 an excellent little museum was opened on the site which helps to explain a good deal about Romans.

They came from various parts of the Empire — at one time Gauls were stationed at Arbeia as well as Tigris lightermen. Two of the finest tombstones found on the wall are here. One is to Victor, a Moorish freedman of Numerianus, a trooper of the Asturians, and another to Regina, aged 30, a British freedwoman and wife of Barates of Palmyra. She is shown sitting in a chair and the stone must have been carved by a Syrian craftsmen. In the museum are models, photographs and plans. Information is provided on different crafts, including the art of writing. There are ornaments, glassware and property.

The most recent addition to the fort is the rebuilding of one of the gateways as it was used in Roman times. It is based on information provided by experts on Roman architecture. Rebuilding is not usual — the only other example is at Vindolanda, though a good deal is done in other countries. Many archaeologists and English Heritage do not like the idea, but this scheme was to be carried out and funded by the Tyne and Wear Museums Service, and approval was obtained. The work was completed in 1988. Here very little of the walls are left — only the foundations, and it was considered necessary to give visitors some idea of the scale of the fortifications. They can see how much higher the gateway stood, having three floor levels. There are the wide double doors, constructed in oak and windows that were shuttered. There were battlements and the roof was tiled. The stone was from the same quarry that the Romans had used, but it was taken from houses of the same stone that were being demolished. The Roman fort itself had been robbed of stone during the centuries, leaving only the foundations that have been revealed by excavation.

Within the Gate Tower, used as a museum, a typical quatermaster's store of the second contury has been reconstructed with all kinds of foodstuffs. There are utensils, pottery, glass, tools, fabrics and weapons. Roman armour and weapons are displayed. At times a live show is put on by modern military men like the Ermine Street Guard. There are local craftsmen who will make Roman pairs of boots. The museum shows what the life of a Roman soldier was like and the various tasks he had to perform. There was a parade ground outside the fort, and some of the skulls of animals found in excavation, showed that they had been used for target practice. The Roman soldiers were responsible for building roads and forts, metal working and mending weapons. It was also most important to have fresh water on the site and baths. There were temples as well, and outside the fort was a vicus or civilian settlment.

The importance of South Shields fort is that it is the only permanent stone built supply base that has been excavated in the Roman Empire. Since South Shields is the haven of our modern pilots and the place of the invention of the lifeboat, it might be appropriate to have a Roman ship reconstructed. Rome was a great naval power and ships were necessary to communications and control.

About 1870 some important pieces of armour were dredged up near Tynemouth bar — the boss and ornament of a shield and the cheek piece of helmet. The boss is a metal plate, rectangular and slightly curved to take the shield, and the raised boss covered the hand of the wearer as he held the grip. The boss is ornamented with an eagle and about it are eight small compartments, each with decoration, including the standards and the sign of a bull — that of the VIIIth legion Augusta. There are also five symbolic human figures, perhaps representing seasons. It has been suggested that these pieces may have come from a wreck. Is there more to be found or has it been dredged and dumped out at sea?

From their hill top look out the pilots of the Tyne keep twenty four hour watch.

The two brick-built navigational beacons still stand — they had to be aligned for entrance. Situated nearby are two replica large cannons of a type that once guarded the harbour mouth of the Tyne.

Perils of the mouth of the Tyne

Great skills were needed to navigate the bar, stretching from the Black Middens to Herd Sands, and on these in 1789, a ship, the *Adventure of Newcastle*, was wrecked and the crew were swept away. This provoked the forming of a committee to set up a commission to design a lifeboat. Two models were submitted, one by Willie Wouldhave and the other by Henry Greathead, but neither was completely satisfactory.

Greathead provided a new model embodying Wouldhave's design and this was accepted. Wouldhave's model is in the South Shields' Museum. The first lifeboat, *(Original)*, was launched January 30 1790, 200 years ago and served for forty years. Full credit for it is now given to Henry Greathead.

Wouldhave died in 1821 and was buried at the parish church, St. Hilda's, where he was parish clerk. A model of his lifeboat hangs in the church, and another is carved on his tombstone. There is a fine memorial to him and Greathead in Ocean Road overlooking the canopy that shelters the second South Shields lifeboat appropriately named *Tyne*. Built in 1833, it saved 1,024 lives before being withdrawn in 1887. We are reminded of ferries and river crossings, often difficult and dangerous.

> *O where is the boatmen, I'll give any money,*
> *And you for your trouble rewarded shall be,*
> *To ferry me over the Tyne to maa honey,*
> *Or scull him across that rough river to me*
>
> From the Folk Song, Water of Tyne

South Shields in History

77. Stormy seas at Tynemouth.

After Roman times a monastery was founded by St Hilda on the site where the present church stands — it was the most likely place. The sea came in further in those days and the Lawe could be cut off. Excavations of the Roman fort showed that on the seaward side sand had blown over the ruins of the buildings. The south 'sheels' were rude huts used by fishermen and the area suffered from

176

Viking raids. After the Norman conquest the area became the property of the Prior and Convent of Durham, which was supplied with fish and salt. Medieval trade was in timber, lead and salt; and ships were always passing. There were some 200 salt pans and the industry flourished. It suffered in the Civil War and declined, but about 1650 Isaac Cookson established glassworks, making flint, plate and window glass. Flint and sand came as ballast in the colliers and coal was mined locally. Celia Fiennes (1698) wrote of her visit.

The river Tyne which runs along to Tinmouth, 5 or 6 miles off which I could see very plaine and the Scheld (South Shields) which is the key of fort at the mouth of the river, which disembouges it self into the sea: all this was in views on this high hill.

From 1720 the first shipyard was established, and between 1820 and 1830 something like a hundred ships were built. A writer of that time reported — *The higher parts of the town are commodious and well built, but the street which stretched along the shore of the river for more than a mile in extent is narrow, crooked and inconvenient. The Ropery walk commands a beautiful view of the batteries and the barracks on the northern shore, which display a striking military scene: whilst on the more distant ground, from the brow of lofty rocks, rise the venerable remains of Tynemouth Priory. Such an assemblage of grand and picturesque objects as here present themselves are seldom found and if viewed when the lofty cliffs are gilded by the evening sun and the dashing billows break over the bar, driving their agitated foam against the precipices, over which the solemn abbey, in the weeds of ruin is, now under the corrosive hand of time, sinking to decay — the effect is powerfully impressive.*

J. M. W. Turner painted such a picture of the Tyne.

The church of St Hilda reflected the growth of South Shields. Between 1810 and 1811 much of it was taken down and rebuilt. The steeple, south and west walls remained and part of the east wall. The interior was gaily redecorated, and it was given new pews. Galleries were added round three sides and the nave and the aisles were separated by cast iron arches and pillars. The marble font of 1675 was by Robert Trollop. In 1764 the tower had been heightened. Only the west wall and tower arch within the church retains a medieval look.

By 1829 Steam ships were being used for river trips and as tugs for sailing vessels. Subsidiary industries on the river provided ropes, chains, anchors and masts for ships. In 1837 the famous Marine College of South Shields was founded by Dr Thomas Winterbottom, and since then it has taken students from all over the world. In 1833 the first railway was built. The old Town Hall of 1768 is an interesting building. It has a domed cupola and open arches supported by Tuscan columns. The open ground floor was used as a market for the sale of butter, eggs and other produce.

By 1830 the population had risen to 17,000 and gas lighting had been installed. In 1832 South Shields had its first Member of Parliament under Earl Grey's Reform Act — Robert Ingham. In 1850 it was granted a Charter of Incorporation and a new Council was formed. Nine councillors were elected from South Shields and Jarrow and six from Westoe. Eight aldermen were chosen and John Clay became the first Mayor. A coat of arms was designed, the central piece being a lifeboat with pilots. The supporters are a sailor for 'courage' and a female figure of 'commerce'. The motto as from the lifeboat was 'Always Ready', and under the date of 1850 the words — Courage, Humanity, Commerce.

At this time the borough had four glass works, fifteen ironworks, four chemical and soda factories, four oil, paint and varnish factories, a pottery, a colliery, a soap factory, three ballast wharves, six timber yards, fourteen staiths and two public railways. From 1852 work was begun to provide a more adequate water supply by the Sunderland and South Shields Water Company. A well was sunk at Fulwell and later came the Cleadon well and reservoir. In 1856 a sewerage scheme was started and street improvements were carried out. In 1864 Jarrow Gasworks were purchased and new railways were established. By 1890 when South Shields became a County Borough, the population was 75,000. In 1890 the North and South Marine Parks were opened and West Park in 1894. The Tynemouth Piers were completed by 1895 and South Shields asserted its right to use the South Pier, which the Tyne Commissioners claimed to control.

Shipbuilding was developing, and in 1880 John Readhead moved to West Docks, and by 1900 he was employing 2,000 workers. In 1859 Tyne Dock was opened at Jarrow Slake, and in 1891 a new coal shipping jetty was constructed. By 1900 South Shields was building 20 ships a year, more than anywhere else in Britain. There were schemes to have a bridge from North to South Shields, but it never happened and so the ferries continued to cross.

The prosperity and pride of the borough is shown in the building of the new Town Hall in the Edwardian era, from 1905 - 1910. The architect was E. F. Petch of London, who was very much in fashion for stately buildings. It has Ionic columns to the entrance with a pedimented portico, carrying sculptured figures. The building is rusticated with pilasters and balustrading above the roof. At the north west corner stands a tall clock tower, having a domed top with supporting pillars and ornamental figures. It is topped, appropriately for a maritime palace, with a golden galleon weather vane. This monumental building has been described as the finest display of civic pride in the county. At the time neither Newcastle or Gateshead could rival it.

In 1964 the new South Shields Marine and Technical College was opened at Westoe by the Duke of Edinburgh, taking over from the old Marine School. New equipment was provided and facilities for the study of navigation, ships and seamanship. This is very important to the area, despite the decline in local shipping. Training for the oil industry and the oil rigs is also provided at South Shields.

There have been developments in the Mill Dam area; the name coming from a small tributary of the Tyne and the Corn Mill there. The inlet was partly filled in to give employment in 1819, and some reclaimed land was used to extend St. Hilda's graveyard. In this area, after South Shields was incorporated in 1850 and had its own customs service, a rather impressive Customs House was opened in 1864, and there was considerable quayside development. There were seaport facilities such as outfitters, boarding houses and public houses for sailors. By the 1960s the area was falling into decay. Many buildings became empty, port facilities and transport had changed. It was thought that the

178

Customs House would have to be knocked down, but it was saved by A. L. M. A. (Arts and Live Music Association), and is being converted into an Arts and Music Centre. There has been restoration on the Quayside including the granite setts of road, over which at one time horse traffic clattered. Some old buildings have become the Mill Dam Workshops. The Seaman's Mission has been restored and public houses updated. Some houses have been built and there is a giant mural beside the Mill Dam showing the recent history of South Tyneside, work done under the Youth Enterprise Programme.

78. Market Place, South Shields.

The Old Town Hall, a Grade I listed building was damaged during the blitz in 1941 and it deteriorated so much that it might have been demolished. However, it was saved and is back into use; the upper floor is a place for exhibitions. The lower open floor is a meeting place and shelter. The Market Bell was placed there, and still rings our over the Market Square to announce the opening of the Market at 10.00 am. There are more than 100 stalls on Market Days selling a great variety of goods. The old 'setts' of Market Square have been restored in the old pattern. At night the Old Town Hall is floodlit and presents a very attractive picture. It has, like many other places in the neighbourhood, including Mill Dam, what are called 'Catherine Cookson Connections'.

This applies also to the Museum, which was built in Ocean Road, 1858-60, originally as the Mechanics Institute. It is now the Museum and Art Gallery,. It was attractively built of brick with some dressings, and consists of three large bays. The central one contains the large arched doorway, and on either side are

179

groups of four round headed windows. Above in each bay are arch enclosed double windows — one to each bay. Within the Catherine Cookson gallery one sees what working class life was like in South Tyneside up to 1929, when Catherine left the area. There are reconstructions of the facade of William Black Street, where she lived, only Cissie Affleck's sweetshop where she spent her halfpennies and a kitchen of the period with an aspidestra in its pot, a plant that survived in grim circumstances

The local History gallery shows how things have changed over three generations. The development of the region is depicted in various ways. There is natural history and the landscape. Shipping and shipbuilding of course figure largely, but also mining and industrial history. Attention is given to different kinds of transport, to social history and to archaeology. There are reminders of famous people, and it might be recorded that Flora Robson, a great actress, was born in Westoe Village in 1905. She was daughter of a Scottish engineer and moved to London as a child, but never forgot the North East nor was forgotten by it.

Among many celebrities, two particularly appeal to me — James Mather and Thomas Marshall. James Mather was born in Newcastle 1799, a son of a shipowner. He was sent to study at Edinburgh University, where he gained honours in both medicine and philosophy. He was also practical and invented a ship's lifeboat which was placed on one of his father's ships, *Mary*. Later when the ship was wrecked, the boat saved the crew. This success prompted the Danish Admiralty to copy it.

He started a wine and spirit merchant's place in Dean Street, South Shields, but became interested in politics and very active in the campaign for Parliamentary Reform. He also got involved in medical matters, ship owning interests and the Navigation Laws.

In 1830 there was a terrible mining disaster at St. Hilda's pit, when fifty two lives were lost. He immediately went down to investigate, and henceforth was deeply involved in the causes of pit accidents. His committee presented a report to the government in 1842. In 1839 he rescued three boys from drowning, and in 1845 after an explosion at Jarrow Pit killed forty miners, he was immediately down and saved several lives. As a member of the Board of Health of South Shields he was continually working for better conditions — street sewers and lighting. He was also employed as a 'trouble shooter' in mines, stopping underground fires, and was often consulted on mining matters. He was also involved in improving the navigation of the Tyne. He died at the Grove, Westoe, 1873 after leading an active and rewarding life.

Thomas Marshall gained fame with his revolutionary ideas in shipbuilding on the Tyne. From 1839 he was concerned with the introduction of steam engines and iron hulls. In thirty years his firm built 109 ships, of which 99 were of iron. He claimed to have built the first steam paddle steamer of the Tyne — *The Star*, although this is disputed, but he did build the first steam collier called *Conside*. A remarkable 214 ton iron screw collier called *Bedlington* which was used for the Blyth Tyne coal trade. It might be called the first container ship, since coal wagons were lowered into the ship full of coal and lifted out at the end of the voyage. He continued to make ships until his retirement and though, not the most powerful or influential of shipbuilders, he deserves special mention as a pioneer.

Another person, a century later, who achieved fame, was James Kirkup, author and poet. Brought up in South Shields from 1920, he eventually became Professor of English Literature at Tohoku University in Japan. Two of his popular books describe his early life in South Shields, *The Only Child* and *Sorrows, Passions and Alarms*.

79. The Mauretania sets out from the Tyne 1906.

Chapter Ten. Conclusion - End of Journey

We have at last reached the end of a long journey from the various sources of the Tyne to the North Sea, and have revealed numerous interesting episodes in history. We have also charted the changes made to the river and the landscape — the effects of man, weather and time.

The river has changed greatly. On 24th August 1843 it was reported — *The tide was so low at the mouth of the Tyne, that a pilot, named Robert Young, waded across the bar from the north side to the south side.*

On 6th September 1846 at the time of another low tide, three pilots walked across in the same way.

Ships depended upon the tide and there was the hazard of hidden rocks. However, the river was dredged and the two piers stretched out like great arms to protect the entrance of vessels. Harbour lights were there to guide them. Larger and larger ships were able to come and go.

It is fascinating to watch the swell of the tide. The waves pound the piers while within the water is comparatively calm. The flow of the river is checked by the tide. When a ship passes out to the sea, it tends to behave like an unruly horse, bucking, prancing and rolling. Looking at the breakers they seem like horses jumping fences on a race-course, and we are reminded of Neptune, the god of the sea, with his horses and trident. The Greeks, a seafaring people, called him Poseidon; and they thought of an everlasting struggle beween the sea and man, assisted by their goddess of wisdom, Athene. The Romans may well have prayed to Minerva when approaching the mouth of the Tyne.

The sea is a difficult element from the land — it is restless, fluctuating and temperamental. Twice a day, moved by the proximity of the moon, it frets and fumes at the cliffs, the rocks and the sands. In turn it conditions the activities of the sea-birds, who wait on the tides. It seems that this enormous natural power should be harnessed to provide electricity and spare the fossil fuels. So much coal has been exported on the tide and so much debris has been deposited in the sea.

Water is taken from the Tyne for human an industrial consumption. It returns in the form of waste and sewage, for so long untreated that the salmon never penetrate the polluted waters. Now great improvements have been made and the fish have returned. But there are still very great dangers to both the sea and the river — from chemicals, farm and factory effluent and oil spillages. Though shipwrecks nowadays are infrequent, they are dangerous because of the size of the vessels involved. It was once asssumed that the salt sea would keep itself clean, but this nonsense and pollution is still at an unacceptable level. Man may not be able to control the sea, but he can poison and kill the life in it.

Lord Byron (1788 - 1824) member of a seafaring family and a lover of the sea, wrote at the end of Childe Harold's Pilgrimage —

> Roll on, thou deep and dark blue Ocean — roll!
> The thousand fleets sweep over thee in vain
> Man marks the earth with ruin — his control
> Stops with the shore: upon the watery plain
> The wrecks are all thy deed, nor doth remain
> A shadow of man's ravage, save his own,
> When for a moment, like a drop of rain
> He sinks into thy depths with bubbling groan
> Without a grave, unknell'd, uncoffin'd and unknown.

Aflred, Lord Tennyson (1809 - 1892) was more optimistic. —

> Sunset and evening star,
> And one clear call for me!
> And may there be no moaning of the bar,
> When I put out to sea,
> But such a tide as moving seems asleep,
> Too full for sound and foam.
> When what which drew from out the boundless deep
> Turns again home.
> Twilight and evening bell,
> And after that the dark!
> And may there be no sadmess or farewell,
> When I embark;
> For though from out our bourne of Time and Place
> The flood may bear me far,
> I hope to see my Pilot face to face
> When I have crossed the bar.

Crossing the Bar.

Reading list

B. Alsopp. *Historic Architecture of Newcastle and Northumberland* 1960.
F. Atkinson. *Victorian Britain — North East.* 1989.
M. F. Barbey. *Civil Engineering Heritage.* 1981.
Thomas Bewick — *A Memoir Ed. Bain.* 1978.
D. Bellamy and B. Quale. *England's last Wilderness.* 1989.
E. Bogg. *Border Country.* 1898.
S. Bonney. *Kielder.*
Bulmer's Directory, 1889.
Catherine Cookson Country.
W. A. Campbell. *The Old Tyneside Chemical Industry.* 1961
B. Charlton. *North Tynedale.*
R. Charlton. *History of Newcastle-upon-Tyne.* 1855.
D. Dougan. *History of N.E. Shipbuilding.*
C. Fraser and K. Emsley. *Tyneside.* 1973.
R. Finch. *Coals from Newcastle.* 1973.
Gateshead Doomsday Book.
L. Hepple. *History of Northumberland and Newcastle.* 1976.
J. Hodgson. *History of Northumberland.*
H. Honeyman. *Northumberland.* 1949.
P. M. Horsley. *Eighteenth Century Newcastle.*
K. Hoole. *Railways N.E. England.* 1965.
T. Hopkins. *Northumberland National Park.*
R. W. Johnson. *The Making of the Tyne.* 1895.
Kielder Forest. 1982.
F. Manders. *History of Gateshead.* 1973.
A. Mackenzie. *View of Northumberland.* 1827.
S. Middlebrook. *Newcastle-upon-Tyne, Its Growth and achievement.* 1968.
S. Middlebrook. *Pictures of Tyneside.* 1969.
Northumberland County History — 15 volumes.
W. J. Palmer. *The Tyne and its Tributaries.* 1882.
N. Pevsner. *Buildings of Northumberland. Buildings of Durham. Buildings of Cumbria.*
H. G. Ramm and others. *Shielings and Bastles.* H.M.S.O. 1970.
A. Rastrick. *The Pennine Dales.* 1968.
R. W. Rennison. *Water to Tyneside.* History of the Newcastle and Gateshead Water Company. 1979.
T. H. Rowland. *People and Places.* 1983. *More People and Places.* 1984.
Miscellany of Newcastle, Northumberland, the Borders and the Seas. 1985.
T. Sharp. *Northumberland.* 1969.
Sykes and Fordyce. *Local Records.*
Sue Shaw. *Bill Quay. Also The North East from the Air.*
R. Simper. *Britain's Maritime Heritage.* 1982.
Tourist Guides from Alston to Tynemouth, especially Gateshead, Newcastle, North Tyneside and South Shields. Thanks to the Authorities.

W. W. Tomlinson. *Comprehsnsive Guide to Northumberland.* 1988.
H. Thorold. *County Durham.* 1980.
Town Teacher Trails and Booklets.
L. Turnbull. *History of Leadmining in N.E. England.* 1975.
L. Turnbull. *Home Sweet Home.* 1967.
P. White. *Portrait of County Durham.* 1971.
G. Whittle. *Carlisle and Newcastle Railway.* 1979.
L. Wilkes and G. Dodds. *Tyneside Clasical.* 1964.
L. Wilkes. *Tyneside Portraits.* 1964.
L. Wilkes. *John Dobson, Architect and Landscape Gardener.* 1980.
P. Winter and others. *Newcastle-upon-Tyne.* 1989.

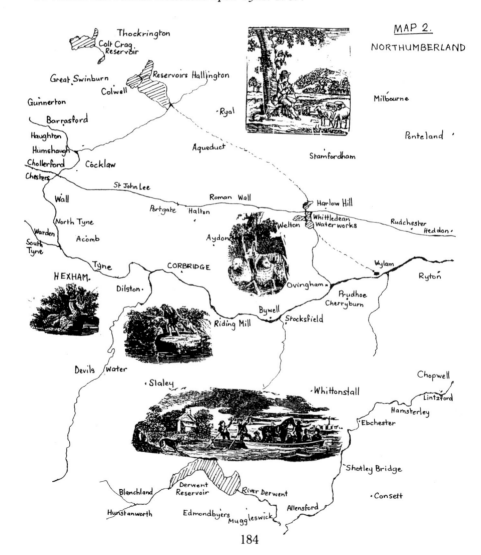

MAP 2.

NORTHUMBERLAND